PRE-
CIVIL
WAR
REFORM

AMERICAN HISTORICAL SOURCES SERIES:
Research and Interpretation

LORMAN RATNER, Editor

PRENTICE-HALL INTERNATIONAL, INC., *London*
PRENTICE-HALL OF AUSTRALIA, PTY. LTD., *Sydney*
PRENTICE-HALL OF CANADA, LTD., *Toronto*
PRENTICE-HALL OF INDIA (PRIVATE) LTD., *New Delhi*
PRENTICE-HALL OF JAPAN, INC., *Tokyo*

Lorman Ratner
Hunter College

PRE-CIVIL WAR REFORM

The Variety of Principles and Programs

Prentice-Hall, Inc., Englewood Cliffs, New Jersey

Current printing (last digit):
10 9 8 7 6 5 4 3 2 1

Library of Congress Catalog Card No.: 67-12238

Printed in the United States of America
C-69500

To Nina and the Children

PREFACE

Pre-Civil War Reform: The Variety of Principles and Programs is a volume in the American Historical Sources Series, devoted to the exploration of aspects of American history and to the process of interpreting historical evidence. The introduction to each volume will be followed by some of the key documents used to prepare the essay. Readers are thus invited to share in the experience of turning raw evidence into history. The essays have been written especially for this series and represent contributions to historical knowledge as well as demonstrations in the writing of history based on sources included in the work.

The word *reform* seems simple enough to define. When we think of reform we think of reshaping; a changing for the better. The years from 1820 to 1860 were an age of reform—a time of significant political, economic, and social change. But why was there such great interest in change in a society that believed itself superior to all others? What made change seem necessary and possible, and how could it be accomplished? The historian seeking answers to these questions has a major task before him. In the introductory essay I have sought to establish certain points of departure in undertaking this task. This essay represents a beginning, not a conclusion.

In even a cursory look at prominent pre-Civil War reformers, the variations in their basic reasons for reform and the variety of their techniques for accomplishing their objectives is striking. Recent studies of reform activity in the progressive era, and even the most elementary study of present reform activity, all disclose variety of principles and programs. This does not mean there are no answers to the questions stated above, but rather that the historian must consider many types of reformers, many principles, and many programs.

LORMAN RATNER

Hunter College

CONTENTS

Introduction

In the decades from 1820 to 1860 Americans devoted much time and money to crusades that were designed to change aspects of their society. Movements aimed at such diverse objectives as ending slavery, prohibiting drinking, morally rehabilitating the poor, establishing women's rights, and converting Jews to Christianity attracted many supporters. Although New Englanders were more responsive than others to these reform appeals, support came from people in all geographical sections and all classes and from both towns and farms. Reform was a national preoccupation.

Recognizing the major role that reform played in the lives of Americans in this era, historians have produced numerous biographies of reform leaders, studies of organizations, and a few syntheses of reform movements in general. The desire to synthesize, coming as it has after a welter of biographies and studies of particular reform movements, has led historians to produce works which add much to our understanding of American reform movements and the impulses behind them. In working out a synthesis, the historian looks for similarities: common motives, personalities working in many reform organizations, common techniques for accomplishing objectives. But synthesizers necessarily must pass over differences; moreover, pre-Civil War reformers' methods and motives varied. There can be no adequate single explanation of why pre-Civil War reform existed, how it operated, or what motivated its participants.

In *Freedom's Ferment*, Alice Felt Tyler, one of the first synthesizers of reform, attributed reform activity to Americans' belief in democracy:

reform was "a declaration of faith in man and in the perfectibility of his institutions."[1] Americans were working toward the goal of the perfect society. The end of the road to utopia, though not yet reached, was close, and reformers would move their society quickly and directly to it. This optimistic belief in perfectibility, attributable to the influence of Enlightenment philosophy and evangelical Protestantism, seemed evident when historians viewed the motives and methods of such reformers as Theodore Parker, William Ellery Channing, or William Lloyd Garrison. But other leaders did not fit into this pattern. John Bodo, in *The Protestant Clergy and Social Issues, 1812-1840,* and Clifford Griffin, in *Their Brothers' Keepers,* among other historians, challenged Miss Tyler's view and instead pictured reformers as men who were concerned with maintaining order in society by establishing or preserving the influence of clergymen or other morally concerned and socially conservative men in power. To these historians, reform in America was an effort to avoid a fall from Grace; it was not a drive to create a godly society but a belief that the godly society was already a fact and that reformers must fight off its attackers. While this explanation accounts for the attitudes and actions of a Lyman Beecher or a Neil Dow and the numerous Protestant clergy involved in reform movements, it leaves no place for the Parkers, Channings, and Garrisons, who, consequently, have been largely ignored by these historians.

Which explanation is correct? Plainly, while both are partly valid, neither is wholly so. In fact, reformers came to their causes from very different backgrounds and with very different motives, which in turn led them to employ different methods. But despite this diversity, there is one factor about which historians agree and which studies of various reformers bear out: *reformers believed God had a plan for America.* This was the era of manifest destiny, of George Bancroft's history of America, in which God always pointed the way. The reformers' belief in a divine plan typified America's belief in such a plan. But what was the plan? How should it be implemented? There was no single

[1] In this and in future volumes, footnotes to the introductory essay will be excluded. The reader will find evidence of the generalizations set forth in the essay in the sources that follow. Students interested in further investigation of a particular point should consult the Suggested Readings list at the conclusion of each volume—L.R.

answer to either question. To some, the divine plan was clear, and the reformers' job was to follow it no matter what the opposition or what fundamental changes in society and institutions had to be made. Others were convinced, however, that the divine plan was already reflected and embedded in American institutions, and that the reformers' primary task was to keep those institutions pure and thus not allow the plan to be subverted. Finally, some reformers, although convinced there was a divine plan, were uncertain as to its content—anxious to please God, yet they were hesitant to pursue a specific course of action.

William Lloyd Garrison was a reformer who believed he understood God's plan perfectly. Northern and southern critics as well as many abolitionists agreed that Garrison was a stubborn, zealous, uncompromising reformer—an anarchist bent on destroying every American institution for the sake of his ideals. In the public's eye, Garrison was the prototype of the abolitionist. Yet Garrison's role in *organized* anti-slavery movements was minor, and his newspaper had few readers. At least part of the explanation for Garrison's uncompromising attitude toward reform was his own view of his role in carrying out the divine plan.

William Lloyd Garrison was convinced that God had revealed this divine plan to him. Garrison saw God as an everpresent force and believed that he and God were in partnership to awaken the conscience of all mankind to sin and, by so doing, dispel all evil. Garrison believed he was the agent appointed to bring the kingdom of God to mankind. Accordingly, he would brook no interference from state, church, or even other reformers.

Garrison clearly stated his role as God's worker in, and in spite of, the American society. Convinced that God was with him, Garrison insisted, from the start, that he was willing to be a martyr to the cause. In 1830, while in a Baltimore jail, the 25-year-old reformer composed a poem in which he revealed this martyr sense:

> Perchance thy fault was love to all mankind;
> Thou didst oppose some vile, oppressive law;
> Or strive all human fetters to unbind;
> Or wouldst not bear the implements of war:—
> . . . A martyr's crown is richer than a King's!

> Think it an honor with thy Lord to bleed,
> And glory midst intensest sufferings!
> Though beat—imprisoned—put to open shame—
> Time shall embalm and magnify thy name.

He wrote in *The Liberator* in 1832:

> But God and His truth, and the rights of man, and the promises of the Holy Scriptures, were with me; and having found a partner whose vision was as clear, whose faith was as strong, and whose self-denial was as great, as my own, I commenced that warfare. . . .

Garrison never lost confidence that he followed the true course. More than thirty years later he assured Edmund Quincy:

> The cause we advocate being not ours, but God's—not ours, but human nature's—appealing to all that is just, human, noble, and true, and upheld by omnipotent arm—it is beyond all defeat, inconquerable and immortal; . . .

This utter confidence kept Garrison immune from the popular sentiment that ran so strongly against him and made him equally intractable when he debated courses of action with fellow abolitionists, who often objected to his perfectionism. Garrison believed that an infinitely merciful God offered salvation to all. Ultimately, all mankind, urged to seek salvation by those who had already been saved, would accept this salvation, and the world would become a perfect place to live. Garrison believed he was ordained to point the way as Christ had first pointed the way to redemption. Actually, slavery was only one of many practices that kept man from following God's will. Garrison championed feminism, the peace crusade, and many other reforms, always seeking to move immediately to the forefront of any organized movement or to start a movement if none existed. With his complete self-righteousness, Garrison took the lead when possible, fought for control, and insisted on dictating policy.

In time, Garrison's tactics and programs alienated other abolitionists. For the first few years after the founding of the New England and American Anti-Slavery Societies, the abolitionists were on good terms, if not united, with one another. Garrison offered abolitionist leader Theodore Weld a position in the New England Anti-Slavery Society, which Weld graciously refused. At an anti-slavery meeting in 1836 both men spoke glowingly of one another, but they had already disagreed, and signs of a break appeared. Garrison made trips to England, where he claimed to speak for American abolitionists, despite his lack of formal position in the American Anti-Slavery Society. In fact, lacking official backing, Garrison had to borrow money from a Negro minister who was in England to solicit funds for a school to teach Negroes trades. New York abolitionists Arthur and Lewis Tappan and Theodore Weld were sponsoring a school for this purpose and felt that Garrison's use of funds was improper. Two years later, Garrison brought English abolitionist George Thompson to America to lecture. At a time when anti-English sentiment in America ran high, many abolitionists considered this to be poor strategy and, indeed, Thompson's appearances often led to rioting.

If Garrison's strategy seemed poorly conceived, his stated views were even more disturbing to many anti-slavery leaders. For its first few years Garrison's newspaper was devoted almost exclusively to anti-slavery, but after the mid-1830's Garrison turned his attention to other causes. First it was women's rights, a cause which many abolitionists rejected. At a time when the anti-slavery movement was facing strong public objections, Garrison was injecting an issue that could lead to internal division. Garrison's success in interesting two South Carolina Quaker sisters, Angelina and Sarah Grimké, in feminism led to a personal dispute between Garrison and Theodore Weld, the latter soon after marrying Angelina Grimké. In 1837 Garrison published a series of letters he had received from the controversial John Humphrey Noyes. Noyes insisted in these letters that any and all institutions that stood in the way of a perfect society must be destroyed. Garrison agreed and soon was crusading for the end of all evils and the elimination of government because it delayed the process of perfecting American and world society. Eventually, Garrison was to make the tearing up of the Constitution a standard part of his platform appearances, and he changed the banner of *The Liberator* to read, "Our Country is the World, Our Countrymen All Mankind. . . ." He announced as a second motto, "Universal Emancipation." This led Weld to write to the New York philanthropist Gerrit Smith that Garrison was in conflict with Jesus and that the continued expression of such views endangered the anti-slavery movement. Another New York abolitionist, Elizur Wright, warned Garrison that his support of many different reform movements would confuse the public and waste reform energies. Wright insisted to Garrison that "Your theory of perfection . . . takes away my hopes of salvation. . . ." Then came the famous anti-slavery convention of 1839 in which Garrison and a boatload of followers came to New York and took control of the American Anti-Slavery Society. Consequently, the New York group withdrew and formed a new society, and Garrison and the New York abolitionists were thus divorced.

Garrison began with no thought of compromise or question as to how he should proceed. Confident that he, as God's agent, would cleanse the world, he was a courageous reformer, but his strength was also his defect. Garrison's rigid belief that his interpretation of God's will was the only correct one made enemies of potential friends. His policies kept him apart from other abolitionists.

But Garrison's was only one interpretation of the divine plan, one view as to how this plan should be implemented. He fought hard, without thought of compromise. Institutions of all sorts would have fallen if he had had his way. Another reformer, Theodore Parker, was a respected minister of an important church, but he was also a figure prominent in Boston's social and political life. Like the seventeenth-century English Puritans, Parker viewed reform as a challenge to moral man working within the bounds of an immoral society.

Parker assumed that God made the natural world perfect and left man to bring the human world into line with the natural. Parker insisted that the God-directed man was entirely on his own in his efforts to reform his world. Though Parker rejected the possibility of supernatural aid, he accepted a supernatural pattern. In a sermon, "The Law of God and the Statutes of Men," Parker made clear the relation between man and God:

> . . . [I]n the human world, man is an actor as well as a tool; he is in part engine, in part also engineer. The ideal of man's conduct, character, and destination resides in God: but thence it is transferred to the mind of man by man's own instinct and reflection: and it is to become actual by man's thought, man's will,

> man's work, . . . This is the dignity of man—he is partial cause and providence of his own affairs.

Garrison saw himself as a divinely appointed prophet who would wage war on evil and somehow destroy it. Parker, although concerned about awakening men to the evil around them, saw evil as both a personal and a social flaw. Man must be moral, but so must society. Moral society would not automatically result from more moral men. Parker tried to reform his world by improving its institutions as well as its individuals, but he never resolved the dilemma of the reformer who accepts both the authority of God and the authority of manmade institutions. Garrison gave no thought to preserving what then existed, but worked to create something new, whereas Parker tried to work within the existing structure. He felt that institutions must not be abandoned and sinners written off as doomed to destruction, and yet there must be no compromise with institutions and no yielding to immoral men.

How could this be done? That was Parker's problem. Parker formed no societies, engaged in no organizational work, but, instead, spoke, wrote, and acted as an individual, using his influence to urge existing powers to reform existing institutions.

Theodore Parker attacked slavery because it was a threat to democratic institutions. He termed slavery an "Oligarchic Idea" which conflicted with the "Democratic Idea." From his pulpit, he cited statistics to prove the economic weakness of the slave system and warned of the political vices apparent in southern life. The Unitarian minister insisted that slavery, in addition to being undemocratic, brought with it violence, atheism, economic ruin, political backwardness, and moral degradation. He declared that the South was determined to maintain its institutions and to spread them into the North, a danger to which Northerners seemed indifferent.

Parker fought slavery from places other than his pulpit. He pressured political leaders to legislate the institution out of existence; he aided fugitive slaves; and plotted with John Brown. Parker resisted the Fugitive Slave Law in every way he could, including resorting to violence. He harbored runaway slaves, successfully spirited one slave away from the authorities, and tried unsuccessfully to free another. For a time, the minister wrote his sermons with a loaded gun on his desk.

When Parker put his anti-slavery plans into action, the contradictions between his theories and his reform programs became apparent. Parker believed that perfection was possible if man would pattern his institutions after God's plan. But despite all his concern for institutions, this reformer had to put himself beyond them. Parker felt that law must be preserved, but it must be moral law as he himself defined it. Garrison, another reformer who cited a higher law, recognized the dilemma here and simply rejected all law except God's, i.e., his own. Parker insisted he stood for law, and yet, at times, he went beyond the law. Garrison insisted that a policy of nonresistance was the best counter to evil laws, but Parker, by his very desire to work within a society of laws, used every means to change them. Garrison renounced the Constitution when he became convinced that it condoned slavery, whereas Parker sought to revise it, at the same time disobeying the Constitution when he was convinced it forced men to oppose God's laws. Although he never admitted it, because of his anti-slavery stand, Parker was close to William Lloyd Garrison's Christian anarchism.

Lyman Beecher, temperance advocate, anti-slavery proponent, and leader of many reform crusades, also believed in a divine plan, a plan which would ultimately result in the kingdom of God on earth. But Beecher assumed that American society was already shaped by that plan, even if it was not yet completely under its influence. God had directed the building of American institutions, and so they ought to be carefully preserved. Admittedly, evil still remained, but like a weed, it had to be eliminated without destroying the healthy plants that grew around it.

Lyman Beecher was introduced to reform through religion. His motives were religious, and his methods were keyed to the theology he espoused. Beecher was trained by the eighteenth-century defender of Calvinism, Timothy Dwight; and Beecher, who became a Congregationalist minister, viewed his struggles against Deism and Unitarianism as a real battle to save souls. In the small New England and New York towns in which he preached, Beecher recognized that the battle against sin was not a contest of theologies alone, but a struggle against certain kinds of social behavior such as dueling and drinking. For Beecher, a born combatant, the war against sin had a social as well as a theological battleground.

After the disestablishment of the Congregational Church in Connecticut, Beecher became increasingly concerned with making religion meaningful to the populace. Beecher stressed the view that although religion was no longer part of the formal body politic, God, through his elect, still governed the world. If men were to be saved, they must accept that rule and follow its dictates. God had his causes, and men had to work for them. Should this divine government be rejected, anarchy and moral destruction would result. With disestablishment, Beecher viewed the role of the minister as a reform leader as crucial to the salvation of America.

Beecher's first major involvement in a reform movement was in temperance work. He felt that if society could be awakened to the evil already wrought by intemperance, men would voluntarily turn away from sin or would awaken souls without threatening institutions. Beecher's series of sermons against drinking was published as *Six Sermons Against Intemperance* and was distributed widely. Like many temperance advocates, Beecher made no attempt to reach drunkards or to work for temperance legislation. Like abolitionists who considered it their primary duty to awaken the non-slaveholding North to the sin of slavery, Beecher sought to awaken sober Americans to the sin of intemperance. For this minister, temperance would help assure that men would be in a condition to receive God's work and respect God's will. As for actual plans to end drinking, the temperance reformer such as Beecher assumed that moral awakening would lead to the rejection of alcohol by the individual's own act.

Beecher's view of the relation of reform to institutions was that once man was morally awakened, he would change his institutions. Beecher rejected both the use of institutions to promote change and the need to destroy institutions because they stood in the way of change. When he became involved in abolition, he rejected Garrison's anti-institutional position and, instead, adopted a position close to that of the Colonizationists. The Colonizationists felt that slavery was immoral and must end, but not at the expense of American institutional stability. The way to accomplish both ends, the Colonizationists argued, was to pay for slaves and then send the freed Negroes back to Africa.

Beecher, like Garrison and Parker, was optimistic in his belief that the divine plan, if properly implemented, would lead Americans to the kingdom of God on earth. But not all religiously motivated reformers were so optimistic. Like others, Maine prohibitionist Neil Dow believed social evil to be the result of sin and was convinced that God's agents had an obligation to fight that sin. But Dow saw no millennium coming, saw no chance that men could be moved purely by moral suasion to abandon evil ways. For Dow, God's agents were assigned the never-ending task of combating evil in order simply to keep society going. Institutionally ordered change, not moral awakening, he felt, was the best weapon. Men must be kept in check or their evil natures, their lust and ignorance, would destroy those institutions, and all barriers to anarchy would be gone.

In a new country the settlers of which faced a wilderness, the problem of assuring order was paramount. The Puritans sought to preserve order by forcing people to remain within the confines of the town where church and civil government could be imposed. But elsewhere the town system was absent, and as settlers spread out across the back country, order depended on voluntary obedience. By the early eighteenth century, the New England town was no longer as effective in this role as it had been, and in some areas, the institutions that maintained order were nonexistent. Some clergy and laymen began to stress the importance of educating the individual to accept a code of behavior even though no institution was present to enforce it. Indeed, advocates of this view sometimes developed a prejudice against institutions and viewed the absence of institutions as a virtue. Benjamin Franklin's simple moralisms, which filled the margins of his *Almanac,* were intended to make Americans orderly without using institutions.

The desire to strike a balance between freedom and order is common to all societies, but, in the first half of the nineteenth century, the tendency to lose this balance seemed to have become especially dangerous in the eyes of men such as Neil Dow. The problem of order in American society, as it came to the fore once again after the War of 1812, seemed to be related to the rapidly changing American society of the time. Geographic and economic mobility along with political change marked the society of the post-war period, and although to many, these factors were virtues, they were also a cause for concern. The temperance interest of men such as Neil Dow must be viewed in the context of this concern.

Dow, the son of a well-to-do merchant and a successful businessman in his own right, was concerned that as his society became more democratic, order would be lost. Politics would become a game of demagogues who would appeal to an uneducated and perhaps intoxicated voting public; workers would lose respect for their employers and, if drunk, would refuse to work, or even attack their superiors. But Dow was more than a conservative who rationalized the preservation of his property and power. It is important to recognize that Dow's concern was for American society, and that his labors reflected more than simple self-interest. Dow entered politics to accomplish his aims. This Maine businessman-politician was an institutionalist, a believer in law and the government that made law and enforced it to maintain balance between freedom and order. In contrast to Weld and Beecher, who believed that moral reformation would allow God's government to rule America and hold the society together, and in contrast to Garrison and Parker, who were willing to set aside human law for the sake of moral progress, Dow felt that all hopes for American society depended on human law and institutions. These motives and beliefs guided Dow's methods for reform.

Neil Dow's initial interest in temperance grew out of his concern that drunk employees often failed to come to work, that they and their families became a social problem, and that at election time, they might easily be swayed by candidates who would buy their votes. To Dow they were the "sort of ignorant and depraved people" who voted for Andrew Jackson. But Dow recognized that drunkenness was not limited to the working class and that the example of prominent citizens drinking hurt any campaign for temperance.

By 1829, Dow had adopted the controversial position of teetotalism and he began to play an active role in the local temperance organization as an advocate of that position. In Maine, as in the rest of the country, the temperance movement was badly divided. One reason for that division was the debate over teetotalism, for many reformers felt that to attack the moderate use of wine would alienate many respectable citizens who might otherwise support the cause. Then there was the split between the Washingtonians, who appealed to drunkards, and the American Temperance Union, which appealed to the non-drunkard—the sober citizen who had to remain that way. Locally, the dispute between these groups was divisive, especially when the Washingtonians, rebuked by the clergy-dominated societies, attacked their religious leaders. Dow tried to ignore such squabbling. He welcomed help from the Washingtonians but rejected any anticlerical position.

He fought for teetotalism but welcomed help from any temperance advocate. With regard to using the power of the state to forbid drinking, Dow rejected both the Washingtonian position that government intervention meant loss of freedom and the clerical view that it constituted an admission of defeat for those who believed reform would come through moral awakening.

Dow had no qualms about using institutions and the power they commanded to accomplish his goal, the orderly society. He became a politician, using temperance as his platform, and he succeeded in becoming prominent in city and later in state politics. It was his acquisition of political power that made it possible, in 1851, for him to push through the first state prohibition law. Most reformers are zealots, and Neil Dow was no exception. In fact, his teetotalism hindered his political career. In politics, where compromise is so vital, Dow, although willing to welcome support from all quarters, was unbending in maintaining his position on temperance. Dow was devoted to the temperance cause as a basis for social order with the same fervor that Beecher was devoted to it as a way of assuring the kingdom of God on earth.

Thus far we have described four reformers, all of whom were moved to action by their belief that some divine plan existed, a plan which they understood and sought to implement. But not all believers in this plan were sure what course of action God intended them to follow. They might even unintentionally oppose God's will. Theodore Weld experienced this dilemma.

Weld saw life as man's continual struggle to escape the full consequences of sin; yet he could not see clearly what sort of works would lead to salvation. He believed that God had a grand design for the universe, but he rejected the possibility that man could ever clearly perceive that design. God called on man to act, but man could not surely know God's will. The road to salvation must be traversed without being clearly seen. Weld wrote his father that reading scripture provided no guide to action unless the reader were in communion with God—a communion Weld described as "subjection and allegiance." Even then, although man might be able to follow, he could "never break a path." God was the pioneer.

Weld believed that God directed him to leave a group of evangelical preachers and devote himself entirely to anti-slavery. In his crusade against slavery, Weld was sure that whatever success he had was because he followed divine will. But in the 1830's, the abolitionists experienced many failures. The public grew more, rather than less, hostile toward abolition: the North joined the South in condemning anti-slavery advocates. In 1834, Weld, bolstered by his belief that God directed him, was still confident. He wrote to abolitionist leader James Birney that "God sits above the storm all undisturbed" and assured Birney that "God is at the helm." A few months later, Weld again wrote his fellow abolitionist to reassure him of God's direction. "May God purify us, gird us for the conflict, give us faith and then we shall stand unscathed by the flames which burn around us."

But Weld became increasingly conscious of his failings and unsure that he correctly understood God's will. His insecurity and hesitation was shown even in his personal life. Just before he wed the abolitionist Angelina Grimké, he wrote her that he felt God might not intend him to marry. Though he made clear his love for her, he remarked that:

> It has often occurred to me that God might have ordered it in His Providence as a *crowning trial* to test my love to Him and see whether I would at His bidding cheerfully relinquish all but Him and for Him.[2]

The wedding took place nonetheless, but such a man could never agitate against slavery with the single-minded self-righteousness of Garrison.

As Weld's anti-slavery career progressed, his letters and his actions reflected his growing uncertainty. Although prominent in the anti-slavery movement, he refused to become an officer in any abolitionist society. Although convinced that slavery was sin, he refused to espouse either Garrison's or Beecher's means for ending it. Weld insisted that once men were awakened to the sinfulness of the institution, God would direct them in steps to end it. Weld's book, *Slavery as It Is,* is a collection of stories of the immorality of slaveholders, whereas the *Bible Against Slavery* made clear the Biblical precedent for rejecting the institution. The reformer assumed that all that was needed to awaken the North to action was an awareness of the sin of slavery. The abolitionist warned his co-workers to avoid answering questions

[2] Italics mine—L.R.

regarding the practical consequences of abolition, for, he insisted, God had not revealed His will on those matters. It was the reformer's job to awaken men to sin, not design plans to eliminate it. Weld and his cohorts, "the seventy," went out to spread the word, but even the northern public failed to heed the message. A few joined the anti-slavery movement, but many stayed away or came only to taunt and throw rocks. From the northern press, pulpit, and political platform came denunciations of abolition. Despite these failures, Weld remained confident. In 1839, six years after he had begun his abolitionist work, he wrote to his wife:

> What God would have me do specifically I as yet have no strong idea, but that He will call to some one particular mode of doing good I have no doubt, . . .

But doubts were in Weld's mind. Switching his tactics from the appeal to personal morality, he agreed to go to Washington to help Joshua Leavitt in his efforts to lobby for anti-slavery measures. While in the Capital, Weld wrote to Angelina: "For more than two years I have ceased to know myself. Terrific visions have risen before me and haunted me everywhere and forever; . . ." In 1840, when James Birney joined a number of leading abolitionists in forming an anti-slavery political party, Weld, suddenly convinced that political action was not God's plan, retired from anti-slavery. He was still the sinner, the half-blind man, waiting for the guiding arm of Providence. Although deeply devoted to anti-slavery and working energetically for the crusade, Weld was even less effective than other contemporary reformers.

Abolitionists have been pictured as cleverly following a plan of attack against slavery; such a generalization is a most inaccurate description of abolitionist Weld. Weld was convinced that God intended to destroy slavery and other evils, but he was never certain how it should be done. Weld was determined to make himself a tool in God's hand, but he was not sure how God wanted to use him. Weld hesitated, shifted from plan to plan, and finally withdrew from reform movements and from society to live an isolated life, leaving America to its fate.

In sum, many reformers of the pre-Civil War era, like many reformers today, came to their causes with the honest righteousness of men determined to do God's bidding. But what was that bidding and how should it be done? A variety of answers led to a variety of reform programs. Although full of zeal, courage, and determination, these early reformers often wasted their energies in debating among themselves. Reform had to be achieved; but if it was part of a divine plan and the reformers were in some way God's agents, the means to the end had to be carefully considered. Debates were understandably vital to these reformers, if seemingly trivial to observers both then and now. They would never have allowed themselves to be discussed together as though they were part of a single movement to reform America. The differences between them were real and were recognized by them; historians must recognize them now. Humanitarianism, democratic liberalism, and religious impulse are legitimate explanations of reform motives, but pre-Civil War reform still defies synthesis. The recognition of variety is the key to pre-Civil War reform, just as it is the key to understanding mid-twentieth-century reform with its advocates of violence, nonviolence, moral awakening, political action, and personal morality.

LORMAN RATNER

Hunter College

part one

WILLIAM LLOYD GARRISON: THE REFORMER AS PERFECTIONIST

Distressed by what seemed to be self-righteousness so evident in Americans' boasts of being superior to all other societies, and especially disturbed by American claims to being the world's freest society, William Lloyd Garrison pointed out time and again the contradiction between our claims and our practices. Slavery seemed clearly to be a denial of the principles of the Declaration of Independence. Since the American government failed to respond to Garrison's demands, he rejected the authority of that government. John Humphrey Noyes's anti-government views bolstered Garrison's own position. For Garrison, anti-slavery became the crusade of the moral, God-directed man against the immoral society. Since neither church nor state would work for abolition, those institutions were subject to Garrison's attacks. These attacks were the logical consequence of the perfectionist view of reform.

source 1

From *The Liberator*

William Lloyd Garrison

We talk of the march of the mind; we marvel at the age of creation; but does knowledge keep pace with ignorance, or virtue with vice, or benevolence with suffering, or liberty with tyranny, among mankind? Most evidently not. How long will it take to regenerate and disenthral benighted Africa? . . . How long to reform republican America? How long to redeem the world?

• • •

In our opinion, nothing but extensive revivals of pure religion can save our country from great plagues and sudden destruction. . . . All reformations whether political, civil, or religious are generally sudden in their nature; they are seldom the result of a momentary excitement, but of a long series of accumulating causes. . . . In proportion as *pure religion* prevails in the land, will the grasp of oppression be weakened, and the liberation of the slaves hastened. Emancipation of the slaves must be the work of Christianity and of the churches: they must achieve the elevation of the blacks, and place them on the equality of the Gospel. . . . Take courage, ye mourning slaves! for your redemption is at hand!

• • •

We aim to overthrow slavery in this country for the following reasons: (1) [it] treats men like property (2) leaves no protection of

William Lloyd Garrison, *The Liberator,* **1,** 1 (January 1, 1831); **1, 15** (April 9, 1831); **3,** 1 (January 1, 1833); and **6,** 1 (January 2, 1836).

person to the slave (3) enemy of virtue, knowledge and religion (4) a system of adultery, prostitution, cruelty, and theft (5) it is the fruitful cause of discord, division and outrage (6) . . . it is contrary to the Declaration of Independence and the Law of God (7) . . . makes slave and master mutual enemies (8) . . . retards prosperity, stains the American name and exposes our land to the severest judgement of heaven.

By immediate emancipation we do not mean: (1) the slaves will be let loose to roam as vagrants (2) that they shall be instantly invested with all political rights and privileges (3) that they shall be expelled from America. But we mean: (1) protection of the law (2) preservation of the family (3) that they will be placed under benevolent supervision until they learn religion and become economically secure.

We hope to be successful in our attempts to abolish slavery—not by encouraging rebellion, nor for the free states to interfere, nor by forcing laws on the South which would be despotism—but by pricking the slaveholders' conscience, by setting public sentiment against slavery through means of press and pulpit.

• • •

It is now a struggle between Right and Wrong—Liberty and Slavery—Christianity and Atheism—Northern Freemen and Southern Taskmasters. The great question to be settled is not whether 2,500,000 slaves in our land shall be immediately or gradually emancipated—or whether they shall be colonized abroad or in our midst—for that is now a subordinate point but whether freedom is with us—THE PEOPLE OF THE UNITED STATES—a reality or a mockery; whether the liberty of speech and of the press . . . is still to be enjoyed. . . . The people—blinded and misled for a time—will in the end see and decide aright. . . . The cause that we espouse is the cause of human liberty.

source 2

From the Letters

William Lloyd Garrison

In the first place, it will be readily admitted, that it is the duty of every nation primarily to administer relief to its own necessities, to cure its own maladies, to instruct its own children, and to watch over its own interests. He is "worse than an infidel" who neglects his own household, and squanders his earnings upon strangers; and the policy of that nation is unwise which seeks to proselyte other portions of the globe at the expense of its safety and happiness. Let me not be misunderstood. My benevolence is neither contracted nor selfish. I pity that man whose heart is not larger than a whole continent. I despise the littleness of that patriotism which blusters only for its own rights, and, stretched to its utmost dimensions, scarcely covers its native territory; which adopts as its creed the right to act independently, even to the verge of licentiousness, without restraint, and to tyrannize wherever it can with impunity. This sort of patriotism is common. I suspect the reality, and deny the productiveness, of that piety which confines its operations to a particular spot—if that spot be less than the whole earth; nor scoops out, in every direction, new channels for the waters of life. Christian charity, while it "begins at home," goes abroad in search of misery. It is as copious as the sun in heaven. It does not, like the Nile, make a partial inundation, and then withdraw; but it perpetually overflows, and fertilizes every barren spot. It is restricted only by the exact number of God's suffering creatures. But I mean to say, that, while we are aiding and instructing foreigners, we ought not to

W. P. Garrison and F. J. Garrison, *William Lloyd Garrison, 1805-1879*, 4 vols. (Boston: Houghton Mifflin Company, 1894), I, 130-37.

forget our own degraded countrymen; that neither duty nor honesty requires us to defraud ourselves that we may enrich others.

The condition of the slaves, in a religious point of view, is deplorable, entitling them to a higher consideration, on our part, than any other race; higher than the Turks or Chinese, for they have the privileges of instruction; higher than the Pagans, for they are not dwellers in a gospel land; higher than our red men of the forest, for we do not bind them with gyves, nor treat them as chattels.

And here let me ask, What has Christianity done, by direct effort, for our slave population? Comparatively nothing. She has explored the isles of the ocean for objects of commiseration; but, amazing stupidity! She can gaze without emotion on a multitude of miserable beings at home, large enough to constitute a nation of freemen, whom tyranny has heathenized by law. In her public services they are seldom remembered, and in her private donations they are forgotten. From one end of the country to the other, her charitable societies form golden links of benevolence, and scatter their contributions like raindrops over a parched heath; but they bring no sustenance to the perishing slave. The blood of souls is upon her garments, yet she heeds not the stain. The clankings of the prisoner's chains strike upon her ear, but they cannot penetrate her heart.

I have said that the claims of the slaves for redress are as strong as those of any Americans could be, in a similar condition. Does any man deny the position? The proof, then, is found in the fact, that a very large proportion of our colored population were born on our soil, and are therefore entitled to all the privileges of American citizens. This is their country by birth, not by adoption. Their children possess the same inherent and unalienable rights as ours, and it is a crime of the blackest dye to load them with fetters.

Every Fourth of July, our Declaration of Independence is produced, with a sublime indignation, to set forth the tyranny of the mother country, and to challenge the admiration of the world. But what a pitiful detail of grievances does this document present, in comparison with the wrongs which our slaves endure! In the one case, it is hardly the plucking of a hair from the head; in the other, it is the crushing of a live body on the wheel—the stings of the wasp contrasted with the tortures of the Inquisition. Before God, I must say, that such a glaring contradiction as exists between our creed and practice the annals of 6000 years cannot parallel. In view of it, I am ashamed of my country. I am sick of our unmeaning declamation in praise of liberty and equality; of our hypocritical cant about the unalienable rights of man. I could not, for my right hand, stand up before a European assembly, and exult that I am an American citizen, and denounce the usurpations of a kingly government as wicked and unjust; or, should I make the attempt, the recollection of my country's barbarity and despotism would blister my lips, and cover my cheeks with burning blushes of shame.

Will this be termed a rhetorical flourish? Will any man coldly accuse me of intemperate zeal? I will borrow, then, a ray of humanity from one of the brightest stars in our American galaxy, whose light will gather new effulgence to the end of time. "This, sirs, is a cause that would be dishonored and betrayed if I contented myself with appealing only to the understanding. It is too cold, and its processes are too slow for the occasion. I desire to thank God that, since he has given me an intellect so fallible, he has impressed upon me an instinct that is sure. On a question of shame and honor—liberty and oppression—reasoning is sometimes useless, and worse. I feel the decision in my pulse: if it throws no light upon the brain, it kindles a fire at the heart. . . ."

I come to my second proposition: the right of the free States to remonstrate against the continuance, and to assist in the overthrow of slavery.

This, I am aware, is a delicate subject, surrounded with many formidable difficulties. But if delay only adds to its intricacy, wherefore shun an immediate investigation? I know that we, of the North, affectedly believe that we have no local interest in the removal of this great evil; that the slave States can take care of themselves, and that any proffered assistance, on our part, would be rejected as impertinent, dictatorial or meddlesome; and that we have no right to lift up even a note of remonstrance. But I believe that these opinions are crude, preposterous, dishonorable, unjust. Sirs, this is a business in which, as members of one great family, we have a common interest; but we take no responsibility, either individually or collectively. Our hearts are cold—our blood stagnates in our veins. We act, in relation to the slaves, as if they were something lower than the brutes that perish.

On this question, I ask no support from the injunction of Holy Writ, which says: "therefore all things whatsoever ye would that men should do to you, do ye even so to them: for this is the law and the prophets." I throw aside the common dictates of humanity. I assert the right of the free States to demand a gradual abolition of slavery, because, by its continuance, they participate in the guilt thereof, and are threatened with ultimate destruction; because they are bound to watch over the interests of the whole country, without reference to territorial divisions; because their white population is nearly double that of the slave States, and the voice of this overwhelming majority should be potential; because they are now deprived of their just influence in the councils of the nation; because it is absurd and anti-republican to suffer property to be represented as men, and *vice versa.*[1] Because it gives the South an unjust ascendancy over other portions of territory, and a power which may be perverted on every occasion. . . .

Now I say that, on the broad system of equal rights, this monstrous inequality should no longer be tolerated. If it cannot be speedily put down—not by force, but by fair persuasion; if we are always to remain shackled by unjust Constitutional provisions, when the emergency that imposed them has long since passed away; if we must share in the guilt and danger of destroying the bodies and souls of men, *as the price of our Union;* if the slave States will haughtily spurn our assistance, and refuse to consult the general welfare; then the fault is not ours if a separation eventually take place. . . .

It may be objected, that the laws of the slave States form insurmountable barriers to any interference on our part.

Answer. I grant that we have not the right, and I trust not the disposition, to use coercive measures. But do these laws hinder our prayers, or obstruct the flow of our sympathies? Cannot our charities alleviate the condition of the slave, and perhaps break his fetters? Can we not operate upon public sentiment, (the lever that can move the moral world), by way of remonstrance, advice, or entreaty? Is Christianity so powerful that she can tame the red men of our forests, and abolish the Burman caste, and overthrow the gods of Paganism, and liberate lands over which the darkness of Superstition has lain for ages;

[1] By the three-fifths representation clause of the Federal Constitution, Art. I., Sec. ii., 3.

and yet so weak, in her own dwelling-place, that she can make no impression upon her civil code? Can she contend successfully with cannibals, and yet be conquered by her own children?

Suppose that, by a miracle, the slaves should suddenly become white. Would you shut your eyes upon their sufferings, and calmly talk of Constitutional limitations? No; your voice would peal in the ears of the taskmasters like deep thunder; you would carry the Constitution by force, if it could not be taken by treaty; patriotic assemblies would congregate at the corners of every street; the old Cradle of Liberty would rock to a deeper tone than ever echoed therein at British aggression; the pulpit would acquire new and unusual eloquence from our holy religion. The argument, that these white slaves are degraded, would not then obtain. You would say, it is enough that they are white, and in bondage, and they ought immediately to be set free. You would multiply your schools of instruction, and your temples of worship, and rely on them for security. . . .

But the plea is prevalent, that any interference by the free States, however benevolent or cautious it might be, would only irritate and inflame the jealousies of the South, and retard the cause of emancipation. If any man believes that slavery can be abolished without a struggle with the worst passions of human nature, quietly, harmoniously, he cherishes a delusion. It can never be done, unless the age of miracles return. No; we must expect a collision, full of sharp asperities and bitterness. We shall have to contend with the insolence, and pride, and selfishness, of many a heartless being. But these can be easily conquered by meekness, and perseverance, and prayer.

Sirs, the prejudices of the North are stronger than those of the South; they bristle, like so many bayonets, around the slaves; they forge and rivet the chains of the nation. Conquer them, and the victory is won. The enemies of emancipation take courage from our criminal timidity. They have justly stigmatized us, even on the floor of Congress, with the most contemptuous epithets. We are (they say) their "white slaves," afraid of our own shadows, who have been driven back to the wall again and again; who stand trembling under their whips; who turn pale, retreat, and surrender, at a talismanic threat to dissolve the Union. . . .

It is often despondingly said, that the evil of slavery is beyond our control. Dreadful conclusion, that puts the seal of death upon our country's existence! If we cannot conquer the monster in his infancy, while his cartilages are tender and his limbs powerless, how shall we escape his wrath when he goes forth a gigantic cannibal, seeking whom he may devour? If we cannot safely unloose two millions of slaves now, how shall we bind upwards of TWENTY MILLIONS at the close of the present century? But there is no cause for despair. We have seen how readily, and with what ease, that horrid gorgon, Intemperance, has been checked in his ravages. Let us take courage. Moral influence, when in vigorous exercise, is irresistible. It has an immortal essence. It can no more be trod out of existence by the iron foot of time, or by the ponderous march of iniquity, than matter can be annihilated. It may disappear for a time; but it lives in some shape or other, in some place or other, and will rise with renovated strength. Let us, then, be up and doing. In the simple and stirring language of the stout-hearted Lundy, "all the friends of the cause must go to work, keep to work, hold on, and never give up."

If it be still objected, that it would be dangerous to liberate the present race of blacks;

I answer—the emancipation of all the slaves of this generation is most assuredly out of the question. The fabric, which now towers above the Alps, must be taken away brick by brick, and foot by foot, till it is reduced so low that it may be overturned without burying the nation in its ruins. Years may elapse before the completion of the achievement; generations of blacks may go down to the grave, manacled and lacerated, without a hope for their children; the philanthropists who are now pleading in behalf of the oppressed, may not live to witness the dawn which will precede the glorious day of universal emancipation; but the work will go on—laborers in the cause will multiply—new resources will be discovered—the victory will be obtained, worth the desperate struggle of a thousand years. Or, if defeat follow, woe to the safety of this people! The nation will be shaken as if by a mighty earthquake. A cry of horror, a cry of revenge, will go up to heaven in the darkness of midnight, and re-echo from every cloud. Blood will flow like water—the blood of guilty men, and of innocent women and children. Then will be heard lamentations and weeping, such as will blot out the remembrance of the horrors of St. Domingo.* The terrible

* Garrison is referring to the great slave revolt there in 1802, an event that both pro- and anti-slavery advocates cited often.

judgments of an incensed God will complete the catastrophe of republican America.

And since so much is to be done for our country; since so many prejudices are to be dispelled, obstacles vanquished, interests secured, blessings obtained; since the cause of emancipation must progress heavily, and meet with much unhallowed opposition, why delay the work? There must be a beginning, and now is a propitious time—perhaps the last opportunity that will be granted us by a long-suffering God. No temporizing, lukewarm measures will avail aught. We must put our shoulders to the wheel, and heave with our united strength. Let us not look coldly on and see our Southern brethren contending single-handed against an all-powerful foe—faint, weary, borne down to the earth. We are all alike guilty. Slavery is strictly a national sin. New England money has been expended in buying human flesh; New England ships have been freighted with sable victims; New England men have assisted in forging the fetters of those who groan in bondage.

I call upon the ambassadors of Christ everywhere to make known this proclamation: "Thus saith the Lord God of the Africans, Let this people go, that they may serve me." I ask them to "proclaim liberty to the captives, and the opening of the prison to them that are bound"—to light up a flame of philanthropy that shall burn till all Africa be redeemed from the night of moral death, and the song of deliverance be heard throughout her borders.

I call upon the churches of the living God to lead in this great enterprise. If the soul be immortal, priceless, save it from remediless woe. Let them combine their energies, and systematize their plans, for the rescue of suffering humanity. Let them pour out their supplications to heaven in behalf of the slave. Prayer is omnipotent: its breath can melt adamantine rocks—its touch can break the stoutest chains. Let anti-slavery charity-boxes stand uppermost among those for missionary, track and educational purposes. On this subject, Christians have been asleep; let them shake off their slumbers, and arm for the holy contest.

I call upon our New England women to form charitable associations to relieve the degraded of their sex. As yet, an appeal to their sympathies was never made in vain. They outstrip us in every benevolent race. Females are doing much for the cause at the South; let their example be imitated, and their exertions surpassed, at the North.

I call upon our citizens to assist in establishing auxiliary colonization societies in every State, county and town. I implore their direct and liberal patronage to the parent society.*

I call upon the great body of newspaper editors to keep this subject constantly before their readers; to sound the trumpet of alarm, and to plead eloquently for the rights of man. They must give the tone to public sentiment. One press may ignite twenty; a city may warm a State; a State may impart a generous heat to a whole country.

I call upon the American people to enfranchise a spot over which they hold complete sovereignty; to cleanse that worse than Augean stable, the District of Columbia, from its foul impurities. I ask them to sustain Congress in any future efforts to colonize the colored population of the States. I conjure them to select those as Representatives who are not too ignorant to know, too blind to see, nor too timid to perform their duty.

I will say, finally, that I despair of the republic while slavery exists therein. If I look up to God for success, no smile of mercy or forgiveness dispels the gloom of futurity; if to our own resources, they are daily diminishing; if to all history, our destruction is not only possible, but almost certain. Why should we slumber at this momentous crisis? If our hearts were dead to every throb of humanity; if it were lawful to oppress, where power is ample; still, if we had any regard for our safety and happiness, we should strive to crush the Vampire which is feeding upon our life-blood. All the selfishness of our nature cries aloud for a better security. Our own vices are too strong for us, and keep us in perpetual alarm; how, in addition to these, shall we be able to contend successfully with millions of armed and desperate men, as we must eventually, if slavery do[es] not cease?

* Garrison soon withdrew his support of the colonization movement.

source 3

From *The Liberator*

William Lloyd Garrison

The motto upon our banner has been, from the commencement of our moral warfare, "OUR COUNTRY IS THE WORLD—OUR COUNTRYMEN ARE ALL MANKIND." We trust that it will be our only epitaph. Another motto we have chosen is, UNIVERSAL EMANCIPATION. Up to this time we have limited its application to those who are held in this country, by Southern taskmasters, as marketable commodities, goods and chattels, and implements of husbandry. Henceforth we shall use it in its widest latitude: the emancipation of our whole race from the dominion of man, from the thraldom of self, from the government of brute force, from the bondage of sin—and bringing them under the dominion of God, the control of an inward spirit, the government of the law of love, and into the obedience and liberty of Christ, who is "*the same,* yesterday, TO-DAY, and forever."

It has never been our design, in conducting the *Liberator*, to require of the friends of emancipation any political or sectarian shibboleth; though, in consequence of the general corruption of all political parties and religious sects, and of the obstacles which they have thrown into the path of emancipation, we have been necessitated to reprove them all. Nor have we any intention—at least, not while ours professes to be an anti-slavery publication, distinctively and eminently—to assail or give the preference to any sect or party. We are bound by no denominational trammels; we are not political partisans; we have taken upon our lips no human creed; we are guided by no human

Quoted in Garrison and Garrison, *William Lloyd Garrison, 1805-1879,* II, 200-204, 302-3.

authority; we cannot consent to wear the livery of any fallible body. The abolition of American slavery we hold to be COMMON GROUND, upon which men of all creeds, complexions and parties, if they have true humanity in their hearts, may meet on amicable and equal terms to effect a common object. But whoever marches on to that ground, loving his creed, or sect, or party, or any worldly interest, or personal reputation or property, or friends, or wife, or children, or life itself, more than the cause of bleeding humanity—or expecting to promote his political designs, or to enforce his sectarian dogmas, or to drive others from the ranks on account of their modes of faith—will assuredly prove himself to be unworthy of his abolition profession, and his real character will be made manifest to all, for severe and unerring tests will be applied frequently: it will not be possible for him to make those sacrifices, or to endure those trials, which unbending integrity to the cause will require. For ourselves, we care not who is found upon this broad platform of our common nature: if he will join hands with us, in good faith, to undo the heavy burdens and break the yokes of our enslaved countrymen, we shall not stop to inquire whether he is a Trinitarian or Unitarian, Baptist or Methodist, Catholic or Covenanter, Presbyterian or Quaker, Swedenborgian or Perfectionist. However widely we may differ in our views on other subjects, we shall not refuse to labor with him against slavery, in the same phalanx, if he refuse not to labor with us. Certainly no man can truly affirm that we have sought to bring any other religious or political tests into this philanthropic enterprise than these: "Thou shalt love thy neighbor as thyself"; "Whatsoever ye would that men should do to you, do ye even so to them"; "Remember those in bonds as bound with them. . . ."

Next to the overthrow of slavery, the cause of PEACE will command our attention. The doctrine of non-resistance as commonly received and practised by Friends, and certain members of other religious denominations, we conceive to be utterly indefensible in its application to national wars—not that it "goes too far," but that it does not go far enough. If a nation may not redress its wrongs by physical force—if it may not repel or punish a foreign enemy who comes to plunder, enslave or murder its inhabitants—then it may not resort to arms to quell an insurrection, or send to prison or suspend upon a gibbet any transgressors upon its soil. If the slaves of the South have not an undoubted right to resist their masters in the last resort, then no man, or body of men, may appeal to the law of violence in self-defence—for none have ever suffered, or can suffer, more than they. If, when men are robbed of their earnings, their liberties, their personal ownership, their wives and children, they may not resist, in no case can physical resistance be allowable, either in an individual or collective capacity.

Now the doctrine we shall endeavor to inculcate is, that the kingdoms of this world are to become the kingdoms of our Lord and of his Christ; consequently, that they are all to be supplanted, whether they are called despotic, monarchical, or republican, and he only who is King of kings, and Lord of lords, is to rule in righteousness. The kingdom of God is to be established IN ALL THE EARTH, and it shall never be destroyed, but it shall "BREAK IN PIECES AND CONSUME ALL OTHERS": its elements are righteousness and peace, and joy in the Holy Ghost: without are dogs, and sorcerers, and whoremongers, and murderers, and idolators, and whatsoever loveth and maketh a lie. Its government is one of love, not of military coercion or physical restraint: its laws are not written upon parchment, but upon the hearts of its subjects—they are not conceived in the wisdom of man, but framed by the Spirit of God: its weapons are not carnal, but spiritual. Its soldiers are clad in the whole armor of God, having their loins girt about with truth, and having on the breastplate of righteousness; their feet are shod with the preparation of the gospel of peace; with the shield of faith they are able to quench all the fiery darts of the wicked, and they wear the helmet of salvation, and wield the sword of the Spirit, which is the word of God. Hence, when smitten on the one cheek, they turn the other also; being defamed, they entreat; being reviled, they bless; being persecuted, they suffer it; they take joyfully the spoiling of their goods; they rejoice, inasmuch as they are partakers of Christ's sufferings; they are sheep in the midst of wolves; in no extremity whatever, even if their enemies are determined to nail them to the cross with Jesus, and if they, like him, could summon legions of angels to their rescue, will they resort to the law of violence.

As to the governments of this world, whatever their titles or forms, we shall endeavor to prove that, in their essential elements, and as at present administered, they are all Anti-Christ; that they can never, by human wisdom, be brought into conformity to the will of God; that they cannot be maintained except by naval and military power; that all their penal enactments, being a dead letter without an army to carry them into effect, are virtually written in human blood; and that the followers of Jesus should instinctively shun their stations of honor, power, and emolument—at the same time "submitting to every ordinance of man, for the Lord's sake," and offering no *physical* resistance to any of their mandates, however unjust or tyrannical. The language of Jesus is, "My kingdom is not of this world, else would my servants fight." Calling his disciples to him, he said to them, "Ye know that they which are accustomed to rule over the Gentiles, exercise lordship over them; and their great ones exercise authority upon them. *But so it* SHALL NOT *be among* YOU; but whosoever will be great among you, shall be your minister; and whosoever of you will be the chiefest, shall be servant of all. For even the Son of man came not to be ministered unto, but to minister, and to give his life a ransom for many."

Human governments are to be viewed as judicial punishments. If a people turn the grace of God into lasciviousness, or make their liberty an occasion for anarchy—or if they refuse to belong to the "one fold and one Shepherd"—they shall be scourged by governments of their own choosing, and burdened with taxation, and subjected to physical control, and torn by factions, and made to eat the fruit of their evil doings, until they are prepared to receive the liberty and the rest which remain, on earth as well as in heaven, for THE PEOPLE OF GOD. This is in strict accordance with the arrangement of Divine Providence.

So long as men contemn the perfect government of the Most High, and will not fill up the measure of Christ's sufferings in their own persons, just so long will they desire to usurp authority over each other—just so long will they pertinaciously cling to human governments, *fashioned in the likeness and administered in the spirit of their own disobedience.* Now, if the prayer of our Lord be not a mockery; if the Kingdom of God is to come universally, and his will to be done ON EARTH AS IT IS IN HEAVEN; and if, in that kingdom, no carnal weapon can be wielded, and swords are beaten into ploughshares, and spears into pruning-hooks, and there is none to molest or make afraid, and no statute-book but the Bible, and no judge but Christ; then why are not Christians obligated to come out NOW, and be separate from "the kingdoms of this world," which are all based upon THE PRINCIPLE OF VIOLENCE, and which require their officers and servants to govern and be governed by that principle? . . .

These are among the views we shall offer in connection with the heaven-originated cause of PEACE—views which any person is at liberty to controvert in our columns, and for which no man or body of men is responsible but ourselves. If any man shall affirm that the anti-slavery cause, as such, or any anti-slavery society, is answerable for our sentiments on this subject, to him may be justly applied the apostolic declaration, "the truth is not in him." We regret, indeed, that the principles of abolitionists seem to be quite unsettled upon a question of such vast importance, and so vitally connected with the bloodless overthrow of slavery. It is time for all our friends to know where they stand. If those whose yokes they are endeavoring to break by the fire and hammer of God's word, would not, in their opinion, be justified in appealing to physical force, how can they justify others of a different complexion in doing the same thing? And if they conscientiously believe that the slaves would be guiltless in shedding the blood of their merciless oppressors, let them say so unequivocally—for there is no neutral ground in this matter, and the time is near when they will be compelled to take sides.

As our object is *universal* emancipation—to redeem woman as well as man from a servile to an equal condition—we shall go for the RIGHTS OF WOMAN to their utmost extent.

. . .

I am quoted, by Mr. Birney,* as "having set the example of voting for a professed abolitionist, and encouraging others to do the same." As to this citation—*cui bono?* I humbly conceive that it concerns no man, or body of men, to know how many or how few times I have voted since the adoption of the A. S. Constitution; or whether I have, or have not, changed my views of politics within a few years. What *I* may have said and done, and what the *Constitution* enjoins, are wholly distinct questions. I deny to no individual abolitionist the right to inculcate the doctrine that it is the religious duty of every man to

* Reference is to James G. Birney, a leader of the American Anti-Slavery Society, and in 1840 Liberty Party candidate for President of the United States.

go to the polls; but when he assumes that the Constitution of the Parent Society maintains that doctrine, and aims to get it endorsed by the Society, as such, in the hope that he shall thus be able to create a schism in the abolition ranks, I pronounce him a disorganizing spirit, however pathetically he may talk about breaking the chains of "the poor slaves," or of his fears that they will be left to perish unless he can succeed in making others swallow his political dogmas.

It is quite remarkable that some of those who have been foremost in protesting against being reckoned my followers—who have been loudest in their boasts that they follow no man—who have been unwilling that I should be regarded as the mouthpiece of the Anti-Slavery Society, in any sense—who have repelled the slightest intimation from the enemies of abolition that the Society is responsible for the sayings and doings of the *Liberator*—I say, it is quite remarkable that all at once, in the eyes of those persons, I have become an official organ, an unerring oracle, the Magnus Apollo of the whole land, whose speech and example are to be followed implicitly—because they have ascertained that, since the year 1833, I have actually voted *once* at the polls! They shall not make me vain. I perceive the design of this incense-offering—to cast me off from the anti-slavery cause, (paradoxical as the statement may seem), in order to secure "the co-operation of the ☞ GREAT MASS OF THE INTELLIGENT MIND [i.e., the aristocracy, the rabbis and scribes] of the nation." I am not willing to be made a tool for their convenience—to be crowned this hour that I may be deposed the next; for it is not true that the *Liberator* has ever been the official journal of any society or body of men, or that any other person, besides its editor, is responsible either for the religious or political sentiments contained in its columns.

source 4

From the Letters

William Lloyd Garrison

W. L. GARRISON TO S. J. MAY, AT BOSTON *

Brooklyn, Dec. 5, 1835

I have just read the scandalous attack upon Miss Martineau,† in the *Daily Advertiser*, to which you refer in your letter. It will confirm her in the faith, for it is too passionate to convince or alarm a steadfast and enlightened mind like hers. To think that the *Advertiser* has at last become so vulgar and malignant as to quote with deference and strong approval the vile slang of the *Courier and Enquirer*! Mr. Hale‡ has lately had a failure in his pecuniary matters, and he now seems to be zealous to become a bankrupt in his editorial character as soon as possible. We ought not to be surprised, however, that the attendance of Miss Martineau at the anti-slavery meeting creates a stir among our opponents, for it is as if a thunderbolt had fallen upon their heads. I believe, could they have foreseen this event, to prevent its occurrence they would have permitted even George Thompson to address the ladies without interruption, and have chosen to sacrifice the honor and glory accruing from a mobocratic victory. It is thus that the wicked are taken

Quoted in Garrison and Garrison, *William Lloyd Garrison, 1805-1879*, II, 56-58, 145-48. [Comments in brackets date from this edition—L.R.]

* Samuel J. May, Unitarian minister from Connecticut and a close friend of Garrison.

† Harriet Martineau, an English writer whose anti-slavery remarks were carried in many northern newspapers.

‡ Nathan Hale, nephew of the Revolutionary War hero and editor of *The Boston Advertiser*.

in their own craftiness, and the counsels of the froward are carried headlong. Surely, it is better to trust in the Lord than to put confidence in princes.

Well, it is announced that the great Dr. Channing* has published his thoughts upon the subject of slavery! Of course, we must now all fall back, and "hide our diminished heads." The book I will not condemn until I peruse it; but I do not believe it is superior either in argument or eloquence to many of our own publications. However, I am heartily glad that he is now committed upon this subject; for, however cautiously and tenderly he may have handled it, if he does not soon have a Southern hornets' nest about his ears, then it will be because hornets have respect unto the persons of men! They will sting him unmercifully, and he will suffer greatly if he is not provided in advance with the genuine abolition panacea. . . .

If the extract from the work [in the *Christian Register*] be a fair sample of the whole of it, it is weak and incoherent enough—indeed, that alone is enough to spoil a good book, especially a book upon moral reform. The Doctor says there are *slaveholders* who "deserve great praise." Why? Because they profess to "deplore and abhor the institution." So did all the slaveholders until they were compelled to tear off their hypocritical mask; and now they go in a body—synods, presbyteries, and all—in open advocacy of the bloody system! But the Doctor's meritorious slaveholders "believe that partial emancipation, in the present condition of society, would bring unmixed evil on bond and free." So do all of them—slave-drivers, slave-traders, and slave-robbers! But these *good* souls further believe, that "they are bound to continue the *relation* [what a nice, soft term!] until it shall be dissolved by comprehensive and systematic measures of the State"! "They are appalled by what seem to them the perils and difficulties of liberating multitudes, born and brought up to that condition"! Here is a mantle of charity (?) broad enough to cover the sin of the world.

I hope uncommon pains will be taken by our abolition brethren to circulate large quantities of this week's *Liberator* before the types are distributed. Bro. Thompson's letter is full of the majesty of truth and the power of love. The defense of his character is most happily

* William Ellery Channing, Boston's most influential Unitarian minister and a leading reformer.

written, and together they ought to traverse the length and breadth of the land.

JOHN HUMPHREY NOYES * TO W. L. GARRISON

Newark, N. J., March 22, 1837

DEAR BR. GARRISON:

In addressing you, I use the liberty which ought to exist between every member of a race which God made of one blood. Moreover, the fact that I was once most heartily engaged in the cause you advocate, and am now separated from it only by devotion to a kindred object, entitles me to call you brother, with peculiar emphasis. When I saw you in Boston, we spoke of the kingdom of God, in its relations to the kingdoms of this world. I rejoiced to find in you a fellowship of views and feelings on this subject which has long been a rarity to me. I proposed to show you a written declaration of my principles, but was prevented. I write now to fulfill that proposal.

I am willing that all men should know that I have subscribed my name to an instrument similar to the Declaration of '76, renouncing all allegiance to the government of the United States, and asserting the title of Jesus Christ to the throne of the world. . . .

When I wish to form a conception of the government of the United States (using a personified representation), I picture to myself a bloated, swaggering libertine, trampling on the Bible—its own Constitution—its treaties with the Indians—the petitions of its citizens: with one hand whipping a [N]egro tied to a liberty-pole, and with the other dashing an emaciated Indian to the ground. On one side stand the despots of Europe, laughing and mocking at the boasted liberty of their neighbor; on the other stands the Devil, saying, "*Esto perpetua.*" In view of such a representation, the question urges itself upon me—"What have I, as a Christian, to do with such a villain?" I live on the territory which he claims—under the protection, to some extent, of the laws which he promulgates. Must I therefore profess to be his friend? God forbid! I will rather flee my country. But every other country is under the same reprobate authority. I must, then,

* Noyes was the founder of the Oneida community. Garrison published a number of letters from Noyes and indicated that he agreed with the perfectionist views set forth. For this reason this letter is included in this section as a statement of Garrison's own position.

either go out of the world, or find some way to live where I am, without being a hypocrite or a partaker in the sins of the nation. I grant that "the powers that be are ordained of God," and this is not less true of individual than of national slaveholders. I am hereby justified in remaining a slave—but not in remaining a slaveholder. Every person who is, in the usual sense of the expression, a citizen of the United States, i.e., a voter, politician, etc., is at once a slave and a slaveholder—in other words, a subject and a ruler in a slaveholding government. God will justify me in the one character, but not in the other. I must therefore separate them and renounce the last. Holding simply the station of a subject, as a Christian I may respect the powers that be, for the Lord's sake, but I cannot make myself a partaker of their ungodly deeds by mingling in their counsels or assisting their operations. "Blessed is the man that walketh not in the counsel of the ungodly, nor standeth in the way of sinners, nor sitteth in the seat of the scornful."

Thus I find a way to "cease to do evil"—now I would "learn to do well." I have renounced active co-operation with the oppressor on whose territories I live; now I would find a way to put an end to his oppression. But he is manifestly a reprobate: reproof and instruction only aggravate his sins. I cannot attempt to reform him, because I am forbidden to "cast pearls before swine." I must therefore either consent to remain a slave till God removes the tyrant, or I must commence war upon him, by a declaration of independence and other weapons suitable to the character of a son of God. I have chosen the latter course for the following reasons:

1. As a believer in the Bible I know that the territory of the United States belongs to God, and is promised, together with the dominion under the whole heaven, to Jesus Christ and his followers.

2. I therefore know that the charter of every government now existing is limited by the will and prediction of him who ordained it; and every nation that expects or hopes for perpetual existence outside of Christ's kingdom is thereby proved guilty of infidelity.

3. By the same authority I know that the nations are to be dashed in pieces before the Kingdom of God can come and [H]is will be done on earth as it is in heaven. The present governments stand in the way of God's kingdom, just as Colonization once stood in the way of Abolition. They occupy the ground, without effecting the object.

4. I regard the existing governments as bearing the same relation to a dispensation that is to come, as that which the Jewish dispensation bore to the Christian—that is, they are preparatory forms of discipline, fitted to the childhood of the race—"shadows of good things to come," which are to be taken away when the substance appears.

5. By the foregoing considerations I am authorized not only to hope for the overthrow of the nations, but to stand in readiness actively to assist in the execution of God's purposes. . . .

6. The Son of God has manifestly, to me, chosen this country for the theatre of such an assault—a country which, by its boasting hypocrisy, has become the laughing-stock of the world, and by its lawlessness has fully proved the incapacity of man for self-government. *My hope of the millennium begins where Dr. Beecher's expires*—VIZ., AT THE OVERTHROW OF THIS NATION.

7. The signs of the times clearly indicate the purpose of God to do his strange work speedily. The country is ripe for a convulsion like that of France; rather, I should say, for the French Revolution reversed. Infidelity roused the whirlwind in France. The Bible, by anti-slavery and other similar movements, is doing the same work in this country. So, in the end, Jesus Christ, instead of a bloodthirsty Napoleon, will ascend the throne of the world. The convulsion which is coming will be, not the struggle of death, but the travail of childbirth—the birth of a ransomed world.

I have stated to you only in the letter the principal things which God has urged upon me by his Spirit, and by which he has moved me to nominate Jesus Christ for the Presidency, not only of the United States, but of the world. Is it not high time for abolitionists to abandon a government whose President has declared war upon them? I cannot but think that many of them hear the same great voice out of heaven which has waked me, saying, "Come out of her[e], my people, that ye be not partakers of her sins and of her plagues." You said your mind was heaving on certain momentous subjects, and you only waited to set anti-slavery in the sunshine before you turned your mind to those subjects. Allow me to suggest that you will set anti-slavery in the sunshine only by making it tributary to Holiness; and you will most assuredly throw it into the shade which now covers Colonization if you suffer it to occupy the ground, in your own mind or in others, which ought to be occupied by UNIVERSAL EMANCIPATION FROM SIN.

All the abhorrence which now falls upon slavery, intemperance, lewdness, and every other specific vice, will in due time be gathered into one volume of victorious wrath against *unbelief*. I wait for that time as for the day of battle, regarding all the previous movements as only fencing-schools and manœuvres of military discipline—or at best as the preliminary skirmishes which precede a general engagement. I counsel you, and the people that are with you, if you love the post of honor—the forefront of the hottest battle of righteousness—to set your face toward *perfect* holiness. Your station is one that gives you power over the nations. Your city is on a high hill. If you plant the standard of perfect holiness where you stand, many will see and flow to it. I judge from my own experience that you will be deserted by many of your present friends; but you will be deserted as Jonah was by the whale—the world, in vomiting you up, will heave you upon the dry land.

source 5

From *The Liberator*

William Lloyd Garrison

Your complaint in the postscript to your letter is, that I "embody abolition," and am "abolition personified and incarnate"—that is, "with some." What do you mean by such language? If nothing more than that my abolition principles are regarded by the friends of immediate emancipation as irrefragably true, then you are in the same predicament with them—for you profess to agree with me in those principles. If you mean (and this is doubtless the "insinuation" you intend to convey), that those who co-operate with me would "swallow" me even if I should abandon the anti-slavery ground—that if I should espouse the Colonization Society they would still obsequiously regard me as "abolition personified and incarnate"—then I have only to repeat that your poisoned arrows are aimed at other bosoms besides my own, and that you are guilty of wholesale calumny. I "embody abolition" just as a thorough-going, consistent temperance-man embodies temperance—and in no other light.

Is it an abolitionist who reproaches me and calumniates others because my advocacy of human rights has been consistent and just, and has won the respect and confidence of a great multitude of good men? How has it happened that I have brought around me, in delightful association, men of all political parties and of all religious sects,

Quoted in Garrison and Garrison, *William Lloyd Garrison, 1805-1879*, II, 155-56. This was written in answer to an attack on Garrison by the Reverend James T. Woodbury and a group of Boston ministers.

notwithstanding the mightiest efforts have been made all over the nation to crush me to the earth, and to make me appear vile in the eyes of the people? It is a problem which has puzzled all the popularity-hunters both in Church and State. But you know something of the rise and progress of the anti-slavery cause, through my humble instrumentality. I was a poor, self-educated mechanic—without important family connexions, without influence, without wealth, without station—patronized by nobody, laughed at by all, reprimanded by the prudent, contemned by the wise, and avoided for a time even by the benevolent. I stood alone, an object of wonder, pity, scorn and malevolence. You can realize nothing of the trials, discouragements and perils through which I have had to pass. The pressure upon me was like an avalanche, and nothing but the power of God sustained me. The clergy were against me—the rulers of the people were against me—the nation was against me. But God and his truth, and the rights of man, and the promises of the Holy Scriptures, were with me; and having found a partner whose vision was as clear, whose faith was as strong, and whose self-denial was as great, as my own, I commenced that warfare which is now going on with such glorious success. From the very first moment that I buckled on my armor, I was assured that I could not maintain my ground; that I should retard instead of aiding the cause of emancipation; that my language was not to be tolerated; that my principles and measures were wild and untenable; and that no person of sane mind would rally under my standard. The entreaties, and warnings, and prophecies, and rebukes which my determination elicited, were numberless; and had I been influenced by them, had not God made my forehead strong against the foreheads of the people, the bark of abolition would have been wrecked upon the rocks and quicksands of human expediency.

I will not stop to trace the progress of this great enterprise. Suffice it to say, that its growth has been such as to astonish nations. Now, sir, if I possess any influence, it has been obtained by being utterly regardless of the opinions of mankind; if I have acquired any popularity, it has been owing to my sturdy unwillingness to seek that honor which comes from men; if I have been "swallowed" by anybody, it is because I have always refused to "confer with flesh and blood." I have flattered no man, feared no man, bribed no man. Yet having made myself of no reputation, I have found a reputation; having refused to be guided by human opinions, I have won "golden opinions" from the best of men; having sought that honor which comes from God, I am not left without honor among my countrymen.

part two

THEODORE PARKER: HUMAN INSTITUTIONS AND DIVINE LAW

By the mid-1850's anti-slavery views were no longer expressed only by a handful of reformers but were stated by many prominent Northerners. Theodore Parker tried to influence the federal government to end slavery despite that government's long history of inaction. At this point Garrison was calling for disunion, but Parker hoped to avoid it. In his sermons against slavery, sermons which were often more secular than theological, Parker sought to reason with his audiences that the individual who is concerned with reconciling the demands of his conscience and his belief in the value of society could reconcile these two and still support anti-slavery. For decades, Garrisonian perfectionist arguments had troubled the naturally conservative majority of the North. Men hesitated to subject all American institutions to the test of moral perfectibility, and so few had been willing to follow Garrison's lead, but Parker hoped through logical persuasion, rather than vitriolic denunciation, to impress on Northerners their guilt in not acting to end slavery and their obligation to themselves and to their society to do so. This, Parker insisted, did not mean destroying institutions but saving them. In the two sermons reprinted here, Parker makes clear how and why this must be done. Note the vast difference between Garrison's journalistic attacks and Parker's lengthy, and at times complex, logic.

source 6

The Function of Conscience

Theodore Parker

It is the function of conscience to discover to men the moral law of God. It will not do this with infallible certainty, for, at its best estate, neither conscience nor any other faculty of man is absolutely perfect, so as never to mistake. Absolute perfection belongs only to the faculties of God. But conscience, like each other faculty, is relatively perfect—is adequate to the purpose God meant it for. It is often immature in the young, who have not had time for the growth and ripening of the faculty, and in the old, who have checked and hindered its development. Here it is feeble from neglect, there from abuse. It may give an imperfect answer to the question, What is absolutely right?

Now, though the conscience of a man lacks the absolute perfection of that of God, in all that relates to my dealing with men, it is still the last standard of appeal. I will hear what my friends have to say, what public opinion has to offer, what the best men can advise me to, then I am to ask my own conscience, and follow its decision; not that of my next friend, the public, or the best of men. I will not say that my conscience will always disclose to me the absolutely right, according to the conscience of God, but it will disclose the relatively right, what is my conviction of right to-day, with all the light I can

Theodore Parker, *Speeches, Addresses and Occasional Sermons* (Boston, 1852). Parker makes numerous references to characters from antiquity and to more modern European and American figures. Identifying notes are provided only when the reader would find it difficult to follow Parker's reasoning without them—L.R.

get on the matter; and as all I can know of the absolute right, is my conviction thereof, so I must be true to that conviction. Then I am faithful to my own conscience, and faithful to my God. If I do the best thing I can know to-day, and to-morrow find a better one and do that, I am not to be blamed, nor to be called a sinner against God, because not so just to-day as I shall be to-morrow. I am to do God's will [as] soon as I know it, not before, and to take all possible pains to find it out; but am not to blame for acting childish when a child, nor to be ashamed of it when grown up to be a man. Such is the function of conscience.

Having determined what is absolutely right, by the conscience of God, or at least relatively right, according to my conscience to-day, then it becomes my duty to keep it. I owe it to God to obey His law, or what I deem His law; that is my duty. It may be uncomfortable to keep it, unpopular, contrary to my present desires, to my passions, to my immediate interests; it may conflict with my plans in life: that makes no difference. I owe entire allegiance to my God. It is a duty to keep His law, a personal duty, my duty as a man. I owe it to myself, for I am to keep the integrity of my own consciousness; I owe it to my brother, and to my God. Nothing can absolve me from this duty, neither the fact that it is uncomfortable or unpopular, nor that it conflicts with my desires, my passions, my immediate interests, and my plans in life. Such is the place of conscience amongst other faculties of my nature.

I believe all this is perfectly plain, but now see what it leads to. In the complicated relations of human life, various rules for the moral conduct of men have been devised, some of them in the form of statute laws, some in the form of customs, and, in virtue of these rules, certain artificial demands are made of men, which have no foundation in the moral nature of man; these demands are thought to represent duties. We have the same word to describe what I ought to do as subject to the law of God, and what is demanded of me by custom, or the statute. We call each a duty. Hence comes no small confusion: the conventional and official obligation is thought to rest on the same foundation as the natural and personal duty. As the natural duty is at first sight a little vague, and not written out in the law book, or defined by custom, while the conventional obligation is well understood, men think that in case of any collision between the two, the natural duty must give way to the official obligation.

For clearness' sake, the natural and personal obligation to keep the law of God as my conscience declares it, I will call Duty; the conventional and official obligation to comply with some custom, keep some statute, or serve some special interest, I will call Business. Here then are two things—my natural and personal duty, my conventional and official business. Which of the two shall give way to the other—personal duty or official business? Let it be remembered that I am a man first of all, and all else that I am is but a modification of my manhood, which makes me a clergyman, a fisherman, or a statesman; but the clergy, the fish, and the State are not to strip me of my manhood. They are valuable insofar as they serve my manhood, not as it serves them. My official business as clergyman, fisherman, or statesman is always beneath my personal duty as man. In case of any conflict between the two, the natural duty ought to prevail and carry the day before the official business; for the natural duty represents the permanent law of God, the absolute right, justice, the balance-point of all interests; while the official business represents only the transient conventions of men, some partial interest; and besides the man who owes the personal duty, is immortal, while the officer who performs the official business, is but for a time. At death, the man is to be tried by the justice of God, for the deeds done, and character attained, for his natural duty, but he does not enter the next life as a clergyman, with his surplice and prayer-book, or a fisherman, with his angles and net, nor yet as a statesman, with his franking privilege, and title of honorable and member of Congress. The officer dies, of a vote or a fever. The man lives forever. From the relation between a man and his occupation, it is plain, in general, that all conventional and official business is to be overruled by natural personal duty. This is the great circle, drawn by God, and discovered by conscience, which girdles my sphere, including all the smaller circles, and itself included by none of them. The law of God has eminent domain everywhere, over the private passions of Oliver and Charles,* the special interests of Carthage and of Rome, over all customs, all official business, all precedents, all human statutes,

* Probably Oliver Cromwell and Charles I.

all treaties between Judas and Pilate, or England and France, over all the conventional affairs of one man or of mankind. My own conscience is to declare that law for me, yours for you, and is before all private passions, or public interests, the decision of majorities, and a world full of precedents. You may resign your office, and escape its obligations, forsake your country, and owe it no allegiance, but you cannot move out of the dominions of God, nor escape where conscience has not eminent domain.

See some examples of a conflict between the personal duty and the official business. A man may be a clergyman, and it may be his official business to expound and defend the creed which is set up for him by his employers, his bishop, his association, or his parish, to defend and hold it good against all comers; it may be, also, in a certain solemn sort, to please the audience, who come to be soothed, caressed, and comforted—to represent the average of religion in his society, and so to bless popular virtues and ban unpopular vices, but never to shake off or even jostle with one of his fingers the load of sin, beloved and popular, which crushes his hearers down till they are bowed together and can in no wise lift themselves up; unpopular excellence he is to call fanaticism, if not infidelity. But his natural duty as a man, standing in this position, overrides his official business, and commands him to tell men of the false things in their creed, of great truths not in it; commands him to inform his audience with new virtue, to represent all of religion he can attain, to undo the heavy burthens of popular sin, private or national, and let the men oppressed therewith go free. Excellence, popular or odious, he is to commend by its own name, to stimulate men to all nobleness of character and life, whether it please or offend. This is his duty, however uncomfortable, unpopular, against his desires, and conflicting with his immediate interests and plans of life. Which shall he do? His official business, and pimp and pander to the public lust, with base compliance serving the popular idols, which here are Money and Respectability, or shall he serve his God? That is the question. If the man considers himself substantially a man, and accidentally a clergyman, he will perform his natural duty; if he counts the priesthood his substance, and manhood an accident of that, he will do only his official business.

I may be a merchant, and my official business may be to buy, and sell, and get gain; I may see that the traffic in ardent spirits is the readiest way to accomplish this. So it becomes my official business to make rum, sell rum, and by all means to induce men to drink it. But presently I see that the common use of it makes the thriving unthrifty, the rich less wealthy, the poor miserable, the sound sick, and the sane mad; that it brings hundreds to the jail, thousands to the alms-house, and millions to poverty and shame, producing an amount of suffering, wretchedness, and sin beyond the power of man to picture or conceive. Then my natural duty as man is very clear, very imperative. Shall I sacrifice my manhood to money?—the integrity of my consciousness to my gains by rum-selling? That is the question. And my answer will depend on the fact, whether I am more a man or more a rum-seller. Suppose I compromise the matter, and draw a line somewhere between my natural duty as man, and my official business as rum-seller, and for every three cents that I make by iniquity, give one cent to the American Tract Society, or the Board for Foreign Missions, or the Unitarian Association, or the excellent Society for promoting the Gospel among the Indians (and others) in North America. That does not help the matter; business is not satisfied, though I draw the line never so near to money; nor conscience, unless the line comes up to my duty.

I am a citizen, and the State says "You must obey all the statutes made by the proper authorities; that is your official business!" Suppose there is a statute adverse to the natural law of God, and the convictions of my own conscience, and I plead that fact in abatement of my obligation to keep the statute, the State says "Obey it, nonetheless, or we will hang you. Religion is an excellent thing in every matter except politics; there it seems to make men mad." Shall I keep the commandment of men, or the law of my God?

A statute was once enacted by King Pharaoh for the destruction of the Israelites in Egypt; it was made the official business of all citizens to aid in their destruction: "Pharaoh charged all his people saying, Every son that is born ye shall cast into the river, and every daughter ye shall save alive." It was the official business of every Egyptian who found a Hebrew boy to throw him into the Nile—if he refused, he offended against the peace and dignity of the kingdom of Egypt, and the form of law in such case made and provided. But if he obeyed, he murdered a man. Which should he obey, the Lord Pharaoh, or the Lord God? That was the question. I make no doubt that the priests of Osiris, Orus, Apis, Isis, and the judges, and the justices of the peace and quorum, and the members of Congress of that time said, "Keep the king's commandment, oh ye that worship the crocodile and fear the cat, or ye shall not sleep in a whole skin any longer!" So said every thing that loveth and maketh a lie. . . .

Last winter a bill for the capture of fugitive slaves was introduced into the Senate of the United States of America; the Senator who so ably represented the opinions and wishes of the controlling men of this city, proposed to support that bill, "with all its provisions to the fullest extent"; that bill, with various alterations, some for the better, others for the worse, has become a law—it received the vote of the Representative from Boston, who was not sent there, I hope, for the purpose of voting for it. That statute allows the slaveholder, or his agent, to come here, and by summary process seize a fugitive slave, and, without the formality of a trial by jury, to carry him back to eternal bondage. The statute makes it the official business of certain magistrates to aid in enslaving a man; it empowers them to call out force enough to overcome any resistance which may be offered, to summon the bystanders to aid in that work. It provides a punishment for anyone who shall aid and abet, directly or indirectly, and harbor or conceal the man who is seeking to maintain his natural and unalienable right to life, liberty and the pursuit of happiness. He may be fined a thousand dollars, imprisoned six months, and be liable to a civil action for a thousand dollars more!

This statute is not to laid to the charge of the slaveholders of the South alone; its most effective supporters are northern men; Boston is more to be blamed for it than Charleston or Savannah, for nearly a thousand persons of this city and neighborhood, most of them men of influence through money if by no other means, addressed a letter of thanks to the distinguished man who had volunteered to support that infamous bill, telling him that he had "convinced the understanding and touched the conscience of the nation." A man falls low when he consents to be a slave, and is spurned for his lack of manhood; to consent to be a catcher of fugitive slaves is to fall lower yet; but to consent to be the defender of a slave-catcher—it is seldom that human nature is base enough for that. But such examples are found in this city! This is now the law of the land. It is the official business of judges, commissioners and marshals, as magistrates, to execute the statute and deliver a fugitive up to slavery; it is your official business and mine, as citizens, when legally summoned, to aid in capturing the man. Does the command make it any man's duty? The natural duty to keep the law of God overrides the obligation to observe any human statute, and continually commands us to love a man and not hate him, to do him justice, and not injustice, to allow him his natural rights not alienated by himself; yes, to defend him in them, not only by all means legal, but by all means moral.

Let us look a little at our duty under this statute. If a man falls into the water and is in danger of drowning, it is the natural duty of the bystanders to aid in pulling him out, even at the risk of wetting their garments. We should think a man a coward who could swim, and would not save a drowning girl for fear of spoiling his coat. He would be indictable at common law. If a troop of wolves or tigers were about to seize a man, and devour him, and you and I could help him, it would be our duty to do so, even to peril our own limbs and life for that purpose. If a man undertakes to murder or steal a man, it is the duty of the bystanders to help their brother, who is in peril, against wrong from the two-legged man, as much as against the four-legged beast. But suppose the invader who seizes the man is an officer of the United States, has a commission in his pocket, a warrant for his deed in his hand, and seizes as a slave a man who has done nothing to alienate his natural rights—does that give him any more natural right to enslave a man than he had before? Can any piece of parchment make right wrong, and wrong right?

The fugitive has been a slave before: does the wrong you committed yesterday give you a natural right to commit wrong afresh and continually? Because you enslaved this man's father, have you a natural right to enslave his child? The same right you would have to murder a man because you butchered his father first. The right to murder is as much transmissible by inheritance as the right to enslave! It is plain to me that it is the natural duty of citizens to rescue every fugitive slave from the hands of the marshal who essays to return him to bondage; to do it peaceably if they can, forcibly if they must, but by all means to do it. Will you stand by and see your countrymen, your fellow-citizens of Boston, sent off to slavery by some commissioner? Shall I see my own parishioners taken from under my eyes and carried back to bondage, by a man whose constitutional business it is to work wickedness by statute? Shall I never lift an arm to protect him? When I consent to that, you may call me a hireling shepherd, an infidel, a wolf in sheep's clothing, even a defender of slave-catching if you will; and I will confess I was a poor dumb dog, barking always at the moon, but silent as the moon when the murderer comes near.

I am not a man who love[s] violence. I respect the sacredness of human life. But this I say, solemnly, that I will do all in my power to rescue any fugitive slave from the hands of any officer who attempts to return him to bondage. I will resist him as gently as I know how, but with such strength as I can command; I will ring the bells, and alarm the town; I will serve as head, as foot, or as hand to any body of serious and earnest men, who will go with me, with no weapons but their hands, in this work. I will do it as readily as I would lift a man out of the water, or pluck him from the teeth of a wolf, or snatch him from the hands of a murderer. What is a fine of a thousand dollars, and jailing for six months, to the liberty of a man? My money perish with me, if it stand between me and the eternal law of God. I trust there are manly men enough in this house to secure the freedom of every fugitive slave in Boston, without breaking a limb or rending a garment.

One thing more I think is very plain, that the fugitive has the same natural right to defend himself against the slave-catcher, or his constitutional tool, that he has against a murderer or a wolf. The man who attacks me to reduce me to slavery, in that moment of attack alienates his right to life, and if I were the fugitive, and could escape in no other way, I would kill him with as little compunction as I would drive a mosquito from my face. It is high time this was said. What grasshoppers we are before the statute of men! what Goliaths against the law of God! What capitalist heeds your statute of usury when he can get illegal interest? How many banks are content with 6 per cent when money is scarce? Did you never hear of a merchant evading the duties of the custom-house? When a man's liberty is concerned, we must keep the law, must we? betray the wanderer, and expose the outcast? [1]

[1] It has been said that the fugitive slave law cannot be executed in Boston. Let us not be deceived. Who would have thought a year ago, that the Senator of Boston would make such a speech as that of last March, that so many of the leading citizens of Boston would write such a letter of

approval, that such a bill could pass Congress, and a man be found in this city (Mr. Samuel A. Eliot) to vote for it and get no rebuke from the people! Yet a single man should not endure the shame alone, which belongs in general to the leading men of the city. The member for Boston faithfully represented the public opinion of his most eminent constituents, lay and clerical. Here is an account of what took place in New York since the delivery of the sermon.

[From the *New York Tribune*]
"Slave Catching in New York—First Case under the Law

"The following case, which occurred yesterday, is one of peculiar interest, from the fact of its being the first case under the new Fugitive Slave Law. It will be noticed that there is very little of the 'law's delay' here; the proceedings were as summary as an Arkansas court audience could desire."

source 7

The Three Chief Safeguards of Society

Theodore Parker

PROVERBS XIV. 34

Righteousness Exalteth a Nation

This is the first Sunday after the anniversary of the national birthday. It seems proper, on this occasion, to go beyond matters merely personal, and affecting us only as individuals. I will speak of the duties of man in a wider sphere; of political affairs. So I ask your attention to a Sermon of the Safeguards of Society. I choose this subject, because some men profess a fear that American society is in danger, and because some persons are busily teaching doctrines which seem hostile to the very design of society itself. I shall not speak of politics as economy, but as morality, and look at the affairs of State from a religious point of view.

We are often told that human society is of divine appointment—society meaning the mass of men living together in a certain fellowship. If this means that man is by nature a social being, and in their progressive development men must unite and form societies, then, it is true, society is of divine appointment. But so is a farm; for man is by nature and position an agricultural being, and in their progressive development men make farms and practise agriculture. Agriculture is as necessary as society. But it does not follow from this, that the Egyptian, the Flemish, or the American mode of agriculture is of divine appoint-

Parker, *Speeches, Addresses and Occasional Sermons.*

ment, and men bound by God to practise that, or to limit themselves thereto; and it no more follows that the Egyptian, the Flemish, or the American mode of society is of divine appointment, and men bound by God to limit themselves to it. It would be thought ridiculous to claim divinity for Dutch farming, or any other special mode of farming; but it is just as ridiculous to claim divinity for Dutch society, or any other society. The farm and the society are alike and equally the work of men.

Then we are often told, that human government is of divine appointment, and men morally bound to submit to it,—government being used as a collective term to include the political, ecclesiastical, and social establishments of a people, and the officers who administer them. If this means, that, at a certain stage of man's progressive political development, it is necessary to have certain political, ecclesiastical, and social establishments, such as a monarchy or an aristocracy, with persons to administer them, then it is true, and government is of divine appointment. But the fence of a farm is just as necessary to agriculture, at a certain stage of agricultural development, as government to society. However, it does not follow from this, that a stone wall or a rail-fence is of divine appointment; and it no more follows that a monarchy or an aristocracy is of divine appointment. It would be thought ridiculous for a farmer to claim divinity for his fence; it is just as absurd for a politician to claim it for his government. Both are alike and equally the work of men.

Again it is said that human statutes are of divine appointment, and therefore binding on the conscience of men. If this means, that, at a certain stage of social and political development, men must form certain rules for social and political conduct, then it is true, and human statutes are of divine appointment. But rules for agricultural conduct are just as necessary for the farm and the garden as political rules for society and the State, and so equally divine. But it does not follow from this, that the agricultural rules for the farm and the garden laid down by Columella* the Roman, or Cobbett † the Briton, are of divine appointment; and it no more follows that the political rules for society and the State laid down by the men of New England or the men of

* Columella (first century A.D.) was a Roman authority on agriculture.

† William Cobbett (early nineteenth century) was an English radical who was concerned, among other things, with government agricultural policies.

New Holland—by men "fore-ordained" at birth to be lawgivers, or by men "elected" in manhood to make laws—are of divine appointment. It would be thought ridiculous for a British farmer to claim divinity for Tusser's "Five Hundred Points of Good Husbandry"; but it is just as absurd for a British politician to claim divinity for the British Constitution, or the statutes of the realm. Rules for farming the land and rules for farming the people are alike and equally the work of men.

Still further, it is said that human officers to execute the statutes, administer the government, and sustain society are also of divine appointment; and hence we are morally bound to employ, honor, and obey them. If this means, that at a certain stage of man's social, political, and legal development, it is necessary to have certain persons whose official business it shall be to execute those statutes, then it is true, and human officers are of divine appointment. But it is just as necessary to have certain persons, whose official business it shall be to execute the rules for farming the land; and so the agricultural officers are just as much of divine appointment as the political. But it does not follow that ploughman Keith and reaper Gibson are such by the grace of God, and therefore we morally bound to employ, honor, and obey them; and it no more follows that King Ferdinand or President Fillmore are such by the grace of God, and we morally bound to employ, honor, and obey them. It would be thought ridiculous for Keith and Gibson to claim divinity for their function of ploughman or reaper; but it is equally absurd for Fillmore and Ferdinand to claim divinity for their function of president or king. The farm-office and the state-office are alike and equally the work of men.

Yet it is often taught that society, government, statutes, and officers are peculiarly and especially of divine appointment, in a very different sense from that mentioned just now; and therefore you and I are morally bound to respect all the four. We are told this by men who would be astonished if any one should claim divine appointment for farm-fences, rules of husbandry, for ploughmen and reapers. This is sometimes done by persons who know no better.

In conformity with that fourfold claim of divinity for things of human appointment, we are told that the great safeguard of man's social welfare is this: Entire subordination of the individual to the community, subordination in mind and conscience, heart and soul; entire submission to the government; entire obedience to the statute;

entire respect for the officer; in short, the surrender of the individual to the State, of his mind to the public opinion, of his conscience to the public statute, of his religion to some bench of attorneys, and his will to the magistrate. This fourfold subordination of the individual is demanded, no matter what the community, the government, the statutes, or the officers may be. Let us look a little more narrowly into this matter, and see what is the purpose, the end, and aim of individual human life, and of social human life; then we may be the better able to determine what are the safeguards thereof.

What is man here on earth to accomplish? He is to unfold and perfect himself, as far as possible, in body and spirit; to attain the full measure of his corporeal and spiritual powers, his intellectual, moral, affectional, and religious powers; to develop the individual into a complete man. That, I take it, is the purpose, the end, the scope, and final cause of individual life on earth. Accordingly, that is the best form of individual life which does this most completely; that worst which does it least. He is the most fortunate man who gets the greatest development of his body and his spirit in all their several and appropriate functions: all else is means thereto, and this the end thereof. Ease, wealth, honor, fame, power, and all the outward things men wish for, and all such things as are valuable, are means to this end, no more Wise men do not account him lucky who comes into the world born to riches, distinction, thrones of power; but him who goes out of it wise, just, good, and holy.

Accordingly, all else is to be subordinated to the attainment of this purpose; this to nothing. But what faculties of the individual are to rule and take precedence? The highest over the lowest; the lasting over the transient; the eternal over the perishing. I will wound my hand to save my head, subordinating the less to the greater. Not barely to live, but to live nobly, is my purpose. I will wound or sacrifice my body to save the integrity of my spirit, to defend the rights of my mind, of my conscience, of my affections, of my religious faculty—my soul. Conscience, when awakened, commands this. Prophets of the Old Testament, and apostles of the New Testament, martyrs of all the churches under heaven, are historical witnesses to this instinct of human nature. Millions of soldiers have been found ready to sacrifice the life of their body to the integrity of their spirit: they would die, but not run.

Man is social by nature: gregarious by instinct, he is social with self-conscious will. To develop the individual into the perfect man, men must mix and mingle. Society is the condition of individual development. Moses or Newton, living all alone, would not have attained the human dignity of a clown or a savage; they would never have mastered articulate speech: the gregarious elephant, the lonely eagle, would surpass these men, born to the mightiest genius. Society, companionship of men, is both a necessity and a comfort, a good in itself, a means to other good.

As the great purpose of human life is to develop the individual into the complete and perfect man in body and spirit, so the purpose of society is to help furnish the means thereto; to defend each, and furnish him an opportunity and all possible help to become a complete and perfect man. Individuals are the monads, the primitive atoms, of which society is composed: its power, its perfection, depend primarily on the power and perfection of the individuals, as much so as the weight of a pendulum or of Mount Sheehallin depends on the primitive atoms thereof. Destroy the individuality of those atoms, human or material—all is gone. To mar the atom is to mar the mass. To preserve itself, therefore, society is to preserve the individuality of the individual.

Such is its general purpose: this involves several particulars. One is purely negative in its form: To prevent men from hurting one another. In early ages, that was the chief business of society which men had become conscious of. Society was recognized as an instrument to help accomplish two things: first, to defend itself against other societies or collections of men, and so preserve the integrity of the mass. This was done by means of armies, forts, fleets, and all the artillery of war. The next thing was, within itself, to defend the many feeble from the few that are strong, or the few strong from the many weak; to preserve the integrity of the individuals, the atoms which compose the mass. This was done by statutes of prohibition, declaring, "Thou shalt not." This defence from foreign or domestic harm involves two things: first, the protection of the person, the substance of the community or the individual; and, next, the protection of the property, the accident of the social or individual person. All this may be comprised in one term as the negative function of society, appearing in two modes, as it protects from foreign or domestic hurt. This function is performed consciously: one community says to other communities, "You shall not hurt me," and to its own members, "You must not hurt one another," and knows what it is about in so doing. Some of the nations of Europe have scarcely got beyond this; their government seems to acknowledge no function but this negative one.

Then comes the positive function of society. That is: To furnish opportunities for the mass, as such, to develop itself; and the individual, as such, to develop himself, individually and socially, and exercise all his faculties in his own way: subject only to this rule, that he hurts nobody else. See how this is done abroad between society and society. This community agrees with others, that they, mutually, shall not only not injure each other, but positively help one another. "Protect my citizens by your statutes, whilst in your land; and I will do the same with yours," says Belgium to France. That is agreed upon. "Let my ships into your harbors," says England, "come whence they may, and with what they may bring; and I will do the same by yours." America says, "Agreed;" and it is so to the good of both. Thus each Christian nation secures for itself opportunities for development in all other Christian countries, and so helps the person, and also his property. This is done by treaties; and each nation has its ministers and consuls to lie abroad, and help accomplish this work. This is the foreign part of the positive function of society, and is destined to a great expansion in times to come.

See how it is done at home, and the whole furnishes positive helps to the special parts. Society establishes almshouses, hospitals, schools, colleges, churches, and postoffices; coins money as a standard measure of all values; builds roads of earth, of water, or of iron; carries letters; surveys the land; prints books telling of its minerals, plants, and living things that swim or creep or fly or walk; puts light-houses along the coast, and breakwaters to protect a port. Thus society furnishes its members a positive help for the mind, body, and estate; helps the individual become a complete and perfect man, by affording him facilities for the development of his substance, and the possession of his accidents. This is the domestic part of the positive function of society. Some men, as the socialists in France, wish to extend it much further, making the government patriarchal to bless—not, as of old, despotic to curse. This also is done with a distinct self-consciousness of the immediate end and the means thereto.

But the greater part of this positive work is done with no such distinct consciousness thereof: it is brought about by the men living together; is done, not by government, but by society. The presence of numbers increases the intellectual temperature, so to say, and quickens the social pulse. Machines are invented, science extended, new truths in morals and religion are found out, literature and art create new loveliness, and men become greater and more noble, while society takes no need; and so all are helped. The government often only checks this work.

By most subtle contrivances, though not of you and me, a provision is made for the great. Without willing it, we prepare a cradle for every giant, ready to receive him soon as he is born. A young woman has a rare genius for music; no legal and constitutional provision has been made for her, society having no instinctive and prophetic consciousness of such an advent; but men with music in their souls, and spell-bound by their ears, are drawn together, and encourage her sweet soul into all the wildest, sweetest, and most bewildering witchery of song. If some lad of marvellous genius is born in the woods, men seek him out, and train him up with the accumulated wisdom of ten thousand years, that this newest diamond from the mine of God may be appropriately set. So it is with a thousand other things; and thus society calls out the dainties of the cook, the machine of the inventor, the orator's persuasive power, the profound thought of the thinker, the poet's vision and his faculty divine, the piety of the highest saint God sends. Thus, [in] spite of all the Herods in Jerusalem, a crown is got ready for him that is born King of the world; wise men are always waiting for the star which goes before the new-born Son of God; and, though that star stand still over a stable, they are ready on the spot with their myrrh, their frankincense, and their gold. Society has its shepherds watching their flock[s], and its angels to proclaim the glad tidings of great joy to all mankind.

While society, in its positive function, thus helps the strong, it provides also for the weak, and gives them the benefit of the strong man's protection: thus the individuality of the ablest and the most feeble is defended at the same time. This is done in part by private charity; in part also by the organized public charity. The sick, the poor, the crazy, the lame, the blind, the deaf, are sacredly cared for. Even the fool is not left in his folly, but the wisdom of society watches over his impotent and wretched brain. Thus the two extremes of the human race are provided for: the man of vast genius and a tough body gets his culture and his place; and from his station in the senate, the pulpit, or the closet, sends out his thunder, his lightning, or his sunshine over all the land, to save the people and to bless; while the lame man, the lunatic woman, the blind boy, the poor and sickly little girl, born with the scrofulous worm feeding on her cheek—all have the benefit of the manifold power of society. The talent of a Webster, the genius of an Emerson, the frailty of an unacknowledged child left on the door-stone at night, to die next month in the almshouse, all have their place in the large cradle of society, whose coverlet wraps them all—the senator, the poet, and the fool. Attend a meeting of the alumni of Harvard College, of the heads of the railroads or factories of New England, a convention of merchants, naturalists, metaphysicians, of the senate of the nation, you see how society gives place and protection to the best heads in the State. Then go to some house of industry, and see the defence afforded for the worst; you see what a wonderful contrivance society itself is. I say a contrivance, yet it is not the contrivance chiefly of Solon or Charlemagne, but of Almighty God; a contrivance for three things: To prevent men from hurting one another in person or property; to give the strong and the weak the advantage of living together; and thus to enable each to have a fair chance for the development of his person and the acquisition of property. The mechanism of society, with its statical and dynamical laws, is the most marvellous phenomenon in the universe. Thereby we are continually building wiser than we know, or rather the providence of the Father builds by us, as by the coral insect of Pacific Seas, foundations for continents which we dream not of.

These three things are the general end of society, and indispensable to the purpose of life. To attain them, there must be a certain amount of individual variety of action, a certain amount of social unity of action; and the two must be to a certain degree balanced into equilibrium. The larger the amount of individual variety and social unity of action, the more complete the equilibrium of the two, the more completely is the purpose of individual and social life accomplished and attained: the atom is not sacrificed to the mass, nor the mass to the atom; the individual gains from being a citizen, the citizen from his individuality; all are the better for each, and each for all.

To accomplish this purpose, men devise certain establishments—institutions, constitutions, statutes—human machinery for attaining the divine end in the individual and the social form. But here is the condition of existence which all these establishments must conform to. Every thing in nature has a certain constant mode of action: this, we call a law of nature. The laws of nature are universal, unchangeable, and perfect as God, whose mind they in part express. To succeed in anything, we must find out and keep the natural laws relating thereto. There are such laws for the individual—constant modes of action which belong to human nature, writ therein by God. My mind and conscience are the faculties by which I learn these laws. Conscience perceives by instinct; mind sees afterwards by experiment. There are also such laws for society, constant modes of action, which belong to human nature in its social form. They are also written in the nature of man. The mind and conscience of the individuals who make up the society are the faculties by which these laws likewise are found out. These laws, constant modes of individual or social action, are the sole and exclusive basis of human establishments which help attain the end of individual and social life. What conforms to these natural rights is called right; what conforms not, is wrong. A mill-dam or a monument must conform to the statical laws of matter, or not serve the purpose it was meant for; a mill or a steam-engine must conform to the dynamical laws of matter, or it is also useless. So all the social establishments of mankind, designed to further the positive or negative functions of society, must conform to the laws of human nature, or they will fail to achieve the purposes of individual and social life.

As I come to individual self-consciousness, I give utterance to these natural laws, or my notion of them, in certain rules of conduct which I make for myself. I say, "This will I do, for it is right; that will I not do, for it is wrong." These are my personal resolutions, personal statutes. I make them in my high act of prayer, and in my common life seek to conform thereto. When I rise higher, in another act of prayer which has a greater experience for its basis and so represents more life, I shall revise the old rules of conduct, and make new ones that are better. The rules of conduct derive all their objective and real value from their conformity with the law of God writ in my nature; all their subjective and apparent value, from their conformity to my notions of the law of God. The only thing which makes it right, and an individual moral duty for me to keep my resolutions, is, that they themselves are right, or I believe them so. Now, as I see they are wrong, or think I see it, I shall revise or change them for better. Accordingly, I revise them many times in my life: now by a gradual change, the process of peaceful development; now by a sudden change, under conviction of sin, in penitence for the past, and great concern of mind for the future, by the process of personal revolution. But these rules of conduct are always provisional—my ladder for climbing up to the purposes of individual life. I will throw them away as soon as I can get better. They are amenable subjectively to my notion of right, and objectively to right itself—to conscience and to God.

As individuals, all, the majority, or some controlling men, come to social self-consciousness, they express these natural laws, or their notion thereof, in certain rules of social conduct. They say, "This shall all men do, for it is right; that shall no man do, for it is wrong." The nation makes its social resolutions, social statutes, in its act of prayer; for legislation is to the State what prayer is to the man—often an act of penitence, of sorrow, of fear, and yet of faith, hope, and love. When it rises higher, it revises and makes better rules of conduct: they derive all their objective and real value from their conformity with the law of God; all their subjective and apparent value, from their conformity with the nation's notion thereof. The only thing which makes it right, and a social moral duty for society, or any of its members, to keep these social statutes, is that they are right, or thought so. In the progress of society, its rules of conduct get revised a good many times: now it is done by gradual, peaceful development; now by sudden and stormy revolutions, when society is penitent for the sin of the past, and in great anxiety and concern of mind through fear of the future. These social statutes are only provisional, to help men climb up to the purpose of social life. They are all amenable subjectively to the notion of right; objectively to right itself—to the conscience of the individuals and to God.

Then society appoints officers whose special conventional function is to see to the execution of these social rules of conduct. They are legally amenable to the rules of conduct they are to carry out; socially amenable to the community that appoints them; individually amenable to their own conscience and to God.

To sum up all this in one formula: Officers are conventionally amenable to society; society, with its officers and its rules of conduct, amenable to the purpose of society; the design of individual life, to the individuals that compose it; individuals, with their rules of conduct, amenable each to his own conscience; and all to the law of the universe, to the Eternal Right, which represents the conscience of God. So far as society is right, government right, statutes right, officers right, all may justly demand obedience from each: for though society, government, statutes, and officers are mere human affairs, as much so as farms, fences, top-dressing, and reapers, and are as provisional as they; yet Right is divine, is of God, not merely provisional and for to-day, but absolute and for eternity. So, then, the moral duty to respect the government, to keep the statutes, to obey the officers, is all resolvable into the moral duty of respecting the integrity of my own nature, of keeping the eternal law of nature, of obeying God. If government, statutes, officers, command me to do right, I must do it, not because commanded, but because it is right; if they command me to do wrong, I must refuse, not because commanded, but because it is wrong. There is a constitution of the universe: to keep that is to preserve the union between man and man, between man and God. To do right is to keep this constitution: that is loyalty to God. To keep my notion of it is loyalty to my own soul. To be false to my notion thereof is treason against my own nature; to be false to that constitution is treason against God. The constitution of the universe is not amenable to men: that is the law of God, the higher law, the constant mode of action of the infinite Father of all. In that He lives and moves, and has His being.

It is now easy to see what are the Safeguards of society, the things which promote the end and aim of society—the development of the body and spirit of all men after their law—and thus help attain the purpose of individual life. I will mention three of these safeguards, in the order of their importance.

First of all, is Righteousness in the People: a religious determination to keep the law of God at all hazards; a sacred and inflexible reverence for right; a determined habit of fidelity each to his own conscience. This, of course, implies a hatred of wrong; a religious and determined habit of disobeying and resisting every thing which contradicts the law of God, of disobeying what is false to this and our conscience. There is no safeguard for society without this. It is to man what impenetrability, with the other primary qualities, is to matter. All must begin with the integral atoms, with the individual mind and conscience; all be tried by that test, personal integrity, at last. What is false to myself I must never do—at no time, for no consideration, in nowise. This is the doctrine of the higher law; the doctrine of allegiance to God; a doctrine which appears in every form of religion ever taught in the world; a doctrine admitted by the greatest writers on the foundation of human law, from Cicero to Lord Brougham.* Even Bentham comes back to this. I know it is now-a-days taught in the United States, that, if any statute is made after the customary legal form, it is morally binding on all men, no matter what the statute may be; that a command to kidnap a black man, and sell him into slavery, is as much morally binding as a command for a man to protect his own wife and child. A people that will practically submit to such a doctrine is not worthy of liberty, and deserves nothing but law, oppressive law, tyrannical law; and will soon get what it deserves. If a people has this notion, that they are morally bound to obey any statute legally made, though it conflict with public morals, with private conscience, and with the law of God, then there is no hope of such a people; and the sooner a tyrant whips them into their shameful grave, the better for the world. Trust me, to such a people the tyrant will soon come. Where the carcass is, thither will the vultures be gathered together. Let no man put asunder the carrion and the crow. So much for the first and indispensable safeguard.

The next is derivative therefrom, Righteousness in the Establishments of the People. Under this name I include three things, namely, institutions, constitutions, and statutes. Institutions are certain modes of operation, certain social, ecclesiastial, or political contrivances for doing certain things. Thus an agricultural club is a social institution to help farming; a private school is a social institution for educating its pupils; a church is an ecclesiastical institution for the promotion of religion; an aristocracy is a political institution for governing all the people by means of a few, and for the sake of a few; a congress of senators and representatives is a legislative institution for making statutes; a jury of twelve men is a judicial institution to help execute the statutes; universal suffrage is a democratic institution for ruling the State.

Constitutions are fundamental rules of conduct for the nation,

* A leader of the middle-class reform movement in England and an avowed abolitionist.

made by the highest human authority in the land, and only changeable thereby, determining what institutions shall be allowed, how administered, by whom and in what manner statutes shall be made.

Statutes are particular rules of conduct to regulate the action of man with man, of individuals with the State, and of the State with individuals.

Statutes are amenable to the constitutions; the constitutions to the institutions; they to the people; all subjectively to the conscience of the individual, and objectively to the conscience of God.

Establishments are the machinery which a people contrives wherewith to carry out its ideas of the right or the expedient. In the present state of mankind, they are indispensable to accomplish the purpose of individual life. There are indeed a few men who for their good conduct, after they are mature, require no human laws whatever. They regulate themselves by their idea of right, by their love of truth, of justice, of man and God. They see the law of God so clear that they need no prohibitive statutes to restrain them from wrong. They will not lie nor steal, though no statutes forbid, and all other men both lie and steal; not if the statutes command falsehood and theft. These men are saints. The wealth of Athens could not make Aristides* unjust. Were all men like Jesus of Nazareth, statutes forbidding wrong would be as needless as sails to a shark, a balloon to a swallow, or a railroad to the lightning of heaven. This is always a small class of men, but one that continually increases. We all look to the time when this will include all men. No man expects to find law books and courts in the kingdom of heaven.

Then there is a class, who need these statutes as a well-known rule of conduct to encourage them to do right, by the assurance that all other men will likewise be made to do so, even if not willing. They see the law of God less clear and strong, and need human helps to keep it. This class comprises the majority of mankind. The court-house helps them, though they never use it; the jail helps them, though never in it. These are common men. They are very sober in Connecticut; not very sober in California.

Then there is a third class who will do wrong, unless they are kept from it by punishment or the fear thereof. They do not see the law of God, or will not keep it if they do. The court-house helps them; so does

* Aristides (520 B.C.-462 B.C.), Athenian statesman, proverbially honest, and called "the just."

the jail, keeping them from actual crime while there, deterring while out of it. Take away the outward restraints, their seeming virtue falls to pieces like a barrel without its hoops. These are knaves. I think this class of men will continually diminish with the advance of mankind; that the saints will grow common, and the knaves get scarce. Good establishments promote this end; those of New England, especially the schools, help forward this good work, to convert the knaves to common men, to transfigure the common men to saints. Bad establishments, like many in Austria, Ireland, and South Carolina, produce the opposite effect: they hinder the development of what is high and noble in man, and call out what is mean and low; for human laws are often instruments to debauch a nation.

If a nation desires to keep the law of God, good establishments will help the work; if it have none such, it must make them before it can be at peace. They are as needful as coats and gowns for the body. Sometimes the consciousness of the people is far in advance of its establishments, and there must be a revolution to restore the equilibrium. It is so at Rome, in Austria and Prussia. All these countries are on the brink of revolution, and are only kept down by the bayonet. It was so here 75 years ago, and our fathers went through fire and blood to get the establishments they desired. They took of the righteousness in the people, and made therefrom institutions, constitutions, and statutes. So much for the second and derivative safeguard.

The third is Righteousness in the Public Officers, good men to administer the establishments, manage the institutions, expound and enforce the constitutions and execute the statutes, and so represent the righteousness of the people. In the hands of such men as see the purpose of social and individual life, and feel their duty to keep the integrity of their conscience and obey the law of God, even bad establishments are made to work well, and serve the purpose of human life; because the man puts out the evil of the institution, constitution, or statute, and puts his own righteousness in its place. There was once a judge in New England who sometimes had to administer bad laws. In these cases, he told the jury, "Such is the law, common or enacted; such are the precedents; such the opinions of Judge This and Judge That; but justice demands another thing. I am bound by my oath as judge to expound to you the law as it is; you are bound by oath as jurors to do justice under it; that is your official business here to-day."

Such a man works well with poor tools; with good ones he would work much better. By the action of such men, aided by public opinion which they now follow and now direct, without any change of legislation, there is a continual progress of justice in the establishments of a nation. Bad statutes are dropped or corrected, constitutions silently ameliorated, all institutions made better. Thus wicked laws become obsolete. There is a law in England compelling all men to attend church. Nobody enforces it.

Put a bad man to administer the establishments, one who does not aim at the purpose of society, nor feel bound to keep the higher law of God, the best institutions, constitutions, statutes, become ineffectual, because the man puts out the good thereof, and puts in his own evil. The best establishments will be perverted to the worst of purposes. Rome had all the machinery of a commonwealth; with Cæsar at the head, it became a despotism. In 1798, France had the establishments of a republic; with Napoleon for first consul, you know what it became: it soon was made an empire, and the Constitution was trodden under foot. In 1851, France has the institutions of a democracy; with Louis Napoleon as chief, you see what is the worth of the provisions for public justice. What was the Constitution of England good for under the thumb of Charles I and James II? What was the value of the common law, of the trial by jury, of Magna Charta, "such a fellow as will have no sovereign," with a George Jeffreys* for judge, a James II for king, and such juries as corrupt sheriffs brought together? They were only a mockery. What were the charters of New England against a wicked king and a corrupt cabinet? Connecticut went out of the court and into the Charter Oak for self-preservation. What were all the institutions of Christianity when Alexander VI † dishonored the seat even of the Pope?

Put a saint, who feels his duty to keep the law of God, in office, even bad rules will work well. But put a man who recognizes no law of God, not into a jail, but in a great office; give him courts and courtiers, fleets and armies, nay, only newspapers and "union committees" to serve him, you see what will be done. The resolute determination of the people to obey the law of God, the righteousness of their establishments, will be of small avail, frustrated by the wickedness of

* During the reign of James II, Jeffreys unfairly judged many accused rebels against the Crown.

† A worldly and aggressive Renaissance Pope.

the men in power. The English Parliament once sent a fleet to aid the Huguenots at Rochelle. King Charles I gave the admiral secret orders to surrender his ships to the enemy he was sent to oppose! The purpose of all human life may be as foully betrayed by wicked men in a high place. In a monarchy, the king is answerable for it with his neck; in a republic there is the same danger; but, where all seems to proceed from the people, it may be more difficult to do justice to a wicked officer. So much for the third safeguard, also derivative from the first.

To make a good house, you want good materials—solid stone, sound bricks, sound timber, a good plan, and also good builders. So, as safeguards of society, to achieve its purpose, you want good material—a righteous people who will be faithful to their own conscience, and obey God and reverence the law of nature; a good plan—righteous establishments, institutions, constitutions, statutes conformable to the laws of God; and you want good builders—righteous officers to represent the eternal justice of the Father. You want this threefold righteousness.

* * *

Such are the safeguards of society; such our condition. What shall we do? Nobody would dare pretend to build a church except on righteousness; that is, the rock of ages. Can you build a State on any other foundation—that house upon the sand? What should you think of a minister of the church who got his deacons together, and made a creed, and said, "There is no higher law; no law of God. You, [l]aymen, must take our word for your guidance, and do just as we bid you, and violate the plainest commands of conscience"? What would be atheism in a minister of the Church—is that patriotism in a minister of the State? A bad law is a most powerful instrument to demoralize and debauch the people. If it is a law of their own making, it is all the worse. There is no real and manly welfare for a man, without a sense of religious obligation to God; none in a family, none in a church, none in a state. We want righteousness in the people, in their establishments, in their officers. I adjure you to reverence a government that is right, statutes that are right, officers that are right; but to disobey everything that is wrong. I entreat you by your love for your country, by the memory of your fathers, by your reverence for Jesus Christ, yea, by the deep and holy love of God which Jesus taught, and you now feel.

part three

LYMAN BEECHER: REFORM AND THE KINGDOM OF GOD

In the letters and part of a sermon that follow, Lyman Beecher makes clear that although church and state are and will be separate in America, the clergy have a responsibility to maintain and improve upon the moral condition of society. Commissioned by God and utilizing both dramatic rhetoric and organized group pressure, these clergy could superimpose a kingdom of God over the secular institutions of the nation. Reform for Beecher was a means to the end of instituting this kingdom. The term *kingdom of God* for Beecher implied both an ultimate coming of the millennium and also a more immediate dominance of moral order. Beecher had no intention of seeking a theocracy—rule by the clergy—in the sense that ministers would utilize the state and govern, but he did see ministers as the leaders in establishing the Godly state, a moral condition, not an institution. Beecher neither ardently defended nor violently attacked institutions, but, rather, neglected the question of moral law versus human law, the question that so concerned Parker.

source 8

From the Letters

Lyman Beecher

MR. BEECHER TO THE REV. ASAHEL HOOKER

Litchfield, July 28, 1812

Without preface, I beg leave to suggest to your consideration a subject which is beginning to be talked upon in these parts. It is that an attempt be made at the ensuing Commencement at New Haven to establish a reformation society for the state. The following considerations have been suggested in favor of such an attempt:

1. The state of public morals, especially with respect to the violation of the Sabbath and the prevalence of intemperance, is such as to demand some special general effort.

2. The providence of God. His judgments call upon us to engage in the work of reformation.

3. A general society would seem to be in many ways adapted to do good; as,

(1) It will tend to awaken the attention of the community to our real state and danger.

(2) Be a rallying-point for all good men.

(3) A general repository of facts as to what needs to be done and the means of doing.

Quoted in Barbara Myers Cross, ed., *The Autobiography of Lyman Beecher* (Cambridge, Mass.: The Belknap Press of Harvard University Press, 1961), I, 185.

(4) It may be the parent and patron of local auxiliary societies, make it easier to establish them, and give them weight and respectability.

(5) May it not be a part of that great and new system of things by which God is preparing to bless the world and fill it with His glory? Who can tell how great a matter a little fire may kindle?

source 9

From the Sermons

Lyman Beecher

Our vices are digging the grave of our liberties, and preparing to entomb our glory. We may sleep, but the work goes on. We may despise admonition, but our destruction slumbereth not. Traveling, and worldly labor, and amusement on the Sabbath will neither produce nor preserve such a state of society as the conscientious observance of the Sabbath has helped to produce and preserve. The enormous consumption of ardent spirit in our land will produce neither bodies nor minds like those which were the offspring of temperance and virtue. The neglect of family government and family prayer, and the religious education of children, will not produce such freemen as were formed by early habits of subordination and the constant influence of the fear of God. . . . Our institutions, civil and religious, have outlived that domestic discipline and official vigilance in magistrates which rendered obedience easy and habitual. The laws are now beginning to operate extensively upon necks unaccustomed to the yoke, and when they shall become irksome to the majority, their execution will become impracticable. To this situation we are already reduced in some districts of the land. Drunkards reel through the streets day after day, and year after year, with entire impunity. Profane swearing is heard, and even by magistrates, as though they heard it not. Efforts to stop traveling on the Sabbath have in all places become feeble, and in many places have

Quoted in Barbara Myers Cross, ed., *The Autobiography of Lyman Beecher* (Cambridge, Mass.: The Belknap Press of Harvard University Press, 1961), I, 191-93; II, 22-25.

wholly ceased. . . . In the meantime, many who lament these evils are augmenting them by predicting that all is lost, encouraging the enemy and weakening the hands of the wise and good. But truly we do stand on the confines of destruction. The mass is changing. We are becoming another people. Our habits have held us long after those moral causes that formed them have ceased to operate. These habits, at length, are giving way. So many hands have so long been employed to pull away foundations, and so few to repair breaches, that the building totters. So much enterprise has been displayed in removing obstructions from the current of human depravity, and so little to restore them, that the stream at length is beginning to run. It may be stopped now, but it will soon become deep, and broad, and rapid, and irresistible. . . .

If we do neglect our duty, and suffer our laws and institutions to go down, we give them up forever. It is easy to relax, easy to retreat, but impossible, when the abomination of desolation has once passed over, to rear again the prostrate altars, and gather again the fragments, and build up the ruins of demolished institutions. . . . We shall become slaves, and slaves to the worst of masters. The profane and the profligate, men of corrupt minds and to every good work reprobate, will be exalted, to pollute us by their example, to distract us by their folly, and impoverish us by fraud and rapine. Let loose from wholesome restraint, and taught sin by the example of the great, a scene most horrid to be conceived, but more dreadful to be experienced, will ensue. No people are more fitted for destruction, if they go to destruction, than we ourselves. All the daring enterprise of our countrymen, emancipated from moral restraint, will become the desperate daring of unrestrained sin. Should we break the bands of Christ, and cast his cords from us, and begin the work of self-destruction, it will be urged on with a malignant enterprise which has no parallel in the annals of time, and be attended with miseries such as the sun has never looked upon. The hand that overturns our laws and altars is the hand of death unbarring the gates of Pandemonium, and letting loose upon our land the crimes and miseries of hell. Even if the Most High should stand aloof and cast not a single ingredient into our cup of trembling, it would seem to be full of superlative woe. But he will not stand aloof. As we shall have begun an open controversy with Him, he will contend openly with us; and never, since the earth stood, has it been so fearful a thing for nations to fall into the hands of the living God. The day of vengeance is in his heart; the day of judgment has come; the great earthquake that is to sink Babylon is shaking the nations, and the waves of the mighty commotion are dashing on every shore.

Is this, then, a time to remove foundations, when the earth itself is shaken? Is this a time to forfeit the protection of God, when the hearts of men are failing them for fear, and for looking after those things which are coming on the earth? Is this a time to run upon his neck and the thick bosses of his buckler, when the nations are drinking blood, and fainting, and passing away in his wrath? Is this a time to throw away the shield of faith, when his arrows are drunk with the blood of the slain; to cut from the anchor of hope, when the clouds are collecting, and the sea and the waves are roaring, and thunders are uttering their voices, and lightnings blazing in the heavens, and great hail is falling upon men, and every mountain, sea, and island is fleeing in dismay from the face of an incensed God?

• • •

EXTRACTS FROM SERMONS

What, then, is this universal, natural, and national remedy for intemperance?

IT IS THE BANISHMENT OF ARDENT SPIRITS FROM THE LIST OF LAWFUL ARTICLES OF COMMERCE BY A CORRECT AND EFFICIENT PUBLIC SENTIMENT, SUCH AS HAS TURNED SLAVERY OUT OF HALF OF OUR LAND, AND WILL YET EXPEL IT FROM THE WORLD.

1825-1860

Nothing should now be said by way of crimination for the past; for verily we have all been guilty in this thing, so that there are few in the land whose brother's blood may not cry out against them from the ground on account of the bad influence which has been lent in some way to the work of destruction.

"We are not, therefore, to come down in wrath upon the distillers, and importers, and vendors of ardent spirits. None of us are enough without sin to cast the first stone; for who would have imported, or distilled, or vended, if all the nominally temperate in the land had refused to drink? It is the buyers who have created the demand for ardent spirits, and made distillation and importation a gainful traffic; and it is the custom of the temperate, too, which inundates the land with the occasion of so much and such unmanageable temptation. Let the temperate cease to buy, and the demand for ardent spirits will fall in the market three-fourths, and ultimately will fail wholly, as the generation of drunkards shall hasten out of time.

To insist that men whose capital is embarked in the production or vending of ardent spirits shall manifest the entire magnanimity and self-denial which is needful to save the land, though the example would be glorious to them, is more than we have a right to expect or demand. Let the consumer do his duty, and the capitalist, finding his employment unproductive, will quickly discover other channels of useful enterprise. All language of impatient censure against those who embarked in the traffic of ardent spirits while it was deemed a lawful calling should therefore be forborne. It would only serve to irritate, and arouse prejudice, and prevent investigation, and concentrate a deaf and deadly opposition against the work of reformation. No *ex post facto* laws. Let us all rather confess the sins which are past, and leave the things which are behind, and press forward in one harmonious attempt to reform the land, and perpetuate our invaluable blessings.

This, however, can not be done effectually so long as the traffic in ardent spirits is regarded as lawful, and is patronized by men of reputation and moral worth in every part of the land. Like slavery, it must be regarded as sinful, impolitic, and dishonorable. That no measures will avail short of rending ardent spirits a contraband of trade is nearly self-evident. . . .

Could all the forms of evil produced in the land by intemperance come upon us in one horrid array, it would appal the nation, and put an end to the traffic in ardent spirit. If, in every dwelling built by blood, the stone from the wall should utter all the cries which the bloody traffic extorts, and the beam out of the timber should echo them back, who would build such a house, and who would dwell in it? What if in every part of the dwelling, from the cellar upward, through all the halls and chambers, babblings, and contentions, and voices, and groans, and shrieks, and wailings, were heard day and night! What if the cold blood oozed out, and stood in drops upon the walls, and, by preternatural art, all the ghastly skulls and bones of the victims destroyed by intemperance should stand upon the walls, in horrid sculpture, within and without the building! Who would rear such a building? What if at eventide and at midnight the airy forms of men destroyed by intemperance were dimly seen haunting the distilleries and stores where they received their bane, or following the track of the ship engaged in the commerce—walking upon the waves, flitting athwart the deck, sitting upon the rigging, and sending up, from the hold within and from the waves without, groans, and loud laments, and wailings? Who would attend such stores? Who would labor in such distilleries? Who would navigate such ships?

Oh! were the sky over our heads one great whispering-gallery, bringing down about us all the lamentation and woe which intemperance creates, and the firm earth one sonorous medium of sound, bringing up around us from beneath the wailings of the damned, whom the commerce in ardent spirit had sent thither—these tremendous realities, assailing our senses, would invigorate our conscience, and give decision to the purpose of reformation. But these evils are as real as if the stone did cry out of the wall, and the beam answered it; as real as if, day and night, wailings were heard in every part of the dwelling, and blood and skeletons were seen upon every wall; as real as if the ghostly forms of departed victims flitted about the ship as she passed over the billows, and showed themselves nightly about stores and distilleries, and with unearthly voices screamed in our ears their loud lament. They are as real as if the sky over our heads collected and brought down about us all the notes of sorrow in the land, and the firm earth should open a passage for the wailings of despair to come up from beneath.

source 10

From His *Autobiography*

Lyman Beecher

Soon after my arrival at Litchfield I was called to attend the ordination at Plymouth of Mr. Heart, ever after that my very special friend. I loved him as he did me. He said to me one day, "Beecher, if you had made the least effort to govern us young men, you would have had a swarm of bees about you; but, as you have come and mixed among us, you can do with us what you will."

Well, at the ordination at Plymouth, the preparation for our creature comforts, in the sitting-room of Mr. Heart's house, besides food, was a broad sideboard covered with decanters and bottles, and sugar, and pitchers of water. There we found all the various kinds of liquors then in vogue. The drinking was apparently universal. This preparation was made by the society as a matter of course. When the Consociation arrived, they always took something to drink round; also before public services, and always on their return. As they could not all drink at once, they were obliged to stand and wait as people do when they go to mill.

There was a decanter of spirits also on the dinner-table, to help digestion, and gentlemen partook of it through the afternoon and evening as they felt the need, some more and some less; and the sideboard, with the spillings of water, and sugar, and liquor, looked

Quoted in Barbara Myers Cross, ed., *The Autobiography of Lyman Beecher* (Cambridge, Mass.: The Belknap Press of Harvard University Press, 1961), I, 179-84.

and smelled like the bar of a very active grog-shop. None of the Consociation were drunk; but that there was not, at times, a considerable amount of exhilaration, I cannot affirm.

When they had all done drinking, and had taken pipes and tobacco, in less than fifteen minutes there was such a smoke you couldn't see. And the noise I can not describe; it was the maximum of hilarity. They told their stories, and were at the height of jocose talk. They were not old-fashioned Puritans. They had been run down. Great deal of spirituality on Sabbath, and not much when they got where there was something good to drink.

I think I recollect some animadversions were made at that time by the people on the amount of liquor drank, for the tide was swelling in the drinking habits of society.

The next ordination was of Mr. Harvey, in Goshen, and there was the same preparation, and the same scenes acted over, and then afterward still louder murmurs from the society at the quantity and expense of liquor consumed.

These two meetings were near together, and in both my alarm, and shame, and indignation were intense. 'Twas that that woke me up for the war. And silently I took an oath before God that I would never attend another ordination of that kind. I was full. My heart kindles up at the thoughts of it now.

There had been already so much alarm on the subject, that at the General Association at Fairfield in 1811, a committee of three had been appointed to make inquiries and report measures to remedy the evil. A committee was also appointed by the General Association of Massachusetts for the same purpose that same month, and to confer with other bodies.

I was a member of General Association which met in the year following at Sharon, June, 1812, when said committee reported. They said they had attended to the subject committed to their care; that intemperance had been for some time increasing in a most alarming manner; but that, after the most faithful and prayerful inquiry, they were obliged to confess they did not perceive that anything could be done.

The blood started through my heart when I heard this, and I rose instantly, and moved that a committee of three be appointed immediately, to report at this meeting the ways and means of arresting the tide of intemperance.

The committee was named and appointed. I was chairman, and on the following day brought in a report, the most important paper that ever I wrote.

ABSTRACT OF REPORT

"The General Association of Connecticut, taking into consideration the undue consumption of ardent spirits, the enormous sacrifice of property resulting, the alarming increase of intemperance, the deadly effect on health, intellect, the family, society, civil and religious institutions, and especially in nullifying the means of grace and destroying souls, recommend:

"1. Appropriate discourses on the subject by all ministers of Association.

"2. That District Associations abstain from the use of ardent spirits at ecclesiastical meetings.

"3. That members of Churches abstain from the unlawful vending, or purchase and use of ardent spirits where unlawfully sold; exercise vigilant discipline, and cease to consider the production of ardent spirits a part of hospitable entertainment in social visits.

"4. That parents cease from the ordinary use of ardent spirits in the family, and warn their children of the evils and dangers of intemperance.

"5. That farmers, mechanics, and manufacturers substitute palatable and nutritious drinks, and give additional compensation, if necessary, to those in their employ.

"6. To circulate documents on the subject, especially a sermon by Rev. E. Porter and a pamphlet by Dr. Rush.*

"7. To form voluntary associations to aid the civil magistrate in the execution of the law.

"And that these practical measures may not be rendered ineffectual,

* Dr. Benjamin Rush published a study of the medical effects of alcoholism, claiming liquor destroyed the innards and even on occasion caused the victim to explode. The description was vivid and frightening.

the Association do most earnestly entreat their brethren in the ministry, the members of our churches, and the persons who lament and desire to check the progress of this evil, that they neither express nor indulge the melancholy apprehension that nothing can be done on this subject; a prediction eminently calculated to paralyze exertion, and become the disastrous cause of its own fulfillment. For what if the reformation of drunkards be hopeless, may we not stand between the living and the dead, and pray and labor with effect to stay the spreading plague? And what if some will perish after all that can be done, shall we make no effort to save any from destruction, because we may not be able to turn away everyone from the path of ruin?

"But how are we assured that nothing can be done? Is it impossible for God to reform and save us? Has He made known His purpose to give us over to destruction? Has He been accustomed to withhold His blessing from humble efforts made to rescue men from the dominion of sin? Have not all past efforts for reformation commenced under circumstances of apparent discouragement, and all great achievements usually begun in little things? The kingdom of heaven was itself, in the beginning, as a grain of mustard-seed, and the apostles, had they consulted appearances only, had never made an effort to enlighten the world.

"Immense evils, we are persuaded, afflict communities, not because they are incurable, but because they are tolerated; and great good remains often unaccomplished merely because it is not attempted.

"If the evil, however, were trivial, or the means of its prevention arduous and uncertain, despondency would be less criminal; but it is a wasting consumption, fastening upon the vitals of society; a benumbing palsy, extending to the extremities of the body; a deep and rapid torrent, bearing the wreck of nations in its course, and undermining rapidly the foundations of our own. It is a case, therefore, of life and death, and what we do must be done quickly, for while we deliberate our strength decays and our foundations totter.

"Let the attention of the public, then, be called up to this subject. Let ministers, and churches, and parents, and magistrates, and physicians, and all the friends of civil and religious order, unite their counsels and their efforts, and make a faithful experiment, and the word and the providence of God afford the most consoling prospect of success.

"Our case is indeed an evil one, but it is not hopeless. Unbelief and sloth may ruin us; but the God of heaven, if we distrust not His mercy, and tempt Him not by neglecting our duty, will help us, we doubt not, to retrieve our condition, and to transmit to our children the precious inheritance received from our fathers.

"The spirit of missions which is pervading the state, and the effusions of the Holy Spirit in revivals of religion, are blessed indications that God has not forgotten to be gracious.

"With these encouragements to exertion, shall we stand idle? Shall we bear the enormous tax of our vices—more than sufficient to support the Gospel, the civil government of the state, and every school and literary institution? Shall we witness around us the fall of individuals—the misery of families—the war upon health and intellect, upon our religious institutions and civil order, and upon the souls of men, without an effort to prevent the evil? Who is himself secure of life in the midst of such contagion? And what evidence have we that the plague will not break into our own families, and that our own children may not be among the victims who shall suffer the miseries of life and the pains of eternal death through our sloth and unbelief?

"Had a foreign army invaded our land to plunder our property and take away our liberty, should we tamely bow to the yoke and give up without a struggle? If a band of assassins were scattering poison, and filling the land with widows and orphans, would they be suffered, without molestation, to extend from year to year the work of death? If our streets swarmed with venomous reptiles and beasts of prey, would our children be bitten and torn to pieces before our eyes, and no efforts made to expel these deadly intruders? But intemperance is that invading enemy preparing chains for us; intemperance is that band of assassins scattering poison and death; intemperance is that assemblage of reptiles and beasts of prey, destroying in our streets the lambs of the flock before our eyes.

"To conclude, if we make a united exertion and fail of the good intended, nothing will be lost by the exertion; we can but die, and it will be glorious to perish in such an effort. But if, as we confidently expect, it shall please the God of our fathers to give us the victory, we may secure to millions the blessings of the life that now is, and the ceaseless blessings of the life to come."

This report was thoroughly discussed and adopted, and a thousand copies ordered to be printed; and that, too, was before people had learned to do much. It was done with zeal and earnestness, such as I had never seen in a deliberative body before.

Dr. Dwight* did indeed say—our father and our friend—that while he approved of our zeal, and appreciated the exigency that called it forth, he was not without some apprehension that in their great and laudable earnestness his young friends might transcend the sanction of public sentiment; but, with a smile peculiarly his own, and heavenly, he added, "If my young friends think it best to proceed, God forbid that I should oppose or hinder them, or withhold my suffrage."

I was not headstrong then, but I was *heartstrong*—oh very, very! I had read and studied everything on the subject I could lay hands on. We did not say a word then about wine, because we thought it was best, in this sudden onset, to attack that which was most prevalent and deadly, and that it was as much as would be safe to take hold of one such dragon by the horns without tackling another; but in ourselves we resolved to inhibit wine, and in our families we generally did.

All my expectations were more than verified. The next year we reported to the Association that the effect had been most salutary. Ardent spirits were banished from ecclesiastical meetings; ministers had preached on the subject; the churches generally had approved the design; the use of spirits in families and private circles had diminished; the attention of the community had been awakened; the tide of public opinion had turned; farmers and mechanics had begun to disuse spirits; the Legislature had taken action in favor of the enterprise; a society for Reformation of Morals had been established, and ecclesiastical bodies in other states had commenced efforts against the common enemy. "The experience of one year had furnished lucid evidence that nothing was impossible to faith."

From that time the movement went on, by correspondence, lec-

* Connecticut's most prominent Congregationalist minister and Beecher's teacher when he was at Yale.

tures, preaching, organization, and other means, not only in Connecticut, but marching through New England, and marching through the world. Glory to God! Oh, how it wakes my old heart up to think of it! though hearts never do grow old, do they? *

* The Massachusetts Temperance Society, the oldest meriting the name, was formed in 1813, as the result of these measures of the Connecticut and Massachusetts Associations. Dr. Rush's "Inquiry into the Effects of Ardent Spirits upon the Human Mind and Body," published in 1804, was the precursor of all subsequent discussions. In February, 1813, Rev. Heman Humphrey, of Fairfield, Connecticut, commenced publishing a series of articles on the subject. Rev. Justin Edwards, of Andover, Massachusetts, commenced preaching on Temperance in 1814. In 1819, Judge Herttell, of New York, published an able "Exposé of the Causes of Intemperate Drinking." The report before the General Association of Connecticut, therefore, stands among the earliest documents of the great Temperance Reformation.

part four

NEIL DOW: ORDER THROUGH REFORM

For Neil Dow, a reform such as temperance was a way of checking individual license for the sake of social order. Garrison viewed reform as a means of freeing the individual from a debilitating social control, while Dow saw the world on the edge of anarchy and feared that it would fall into chaos. Dow did not hesitate to call on society to deprive the individual of his right to drink. Not only did drinking ruin a man morally and economically, but it made him politically irrational, and it destroyed his family life. Dow assumed God wished him to save society.

source 11

From *The Reminiscences*

Neil Dow

Testimony might be adduced indefinitely, tending to show the vast extent of the liquor-traffic and the resulting evils in Maine before the enactment of the prohibitory law. There are few now living acquainted with Maine in those days, and those who know it now and are familiar with its abounding evidences of thrift can hardly understand what it was then. No person could fail to notice the general poverty of the state, and no thoughtful person could fail to connect cause and effect, and to see that much of this poverty was the direct result of the general distribution of the traffic in liquor.

It is not to be understood from that general description of conditions in early Maine that all, or a major part, of her people were suffering from their own excessive indulgence in intoxicants. Such was by no means the case, but all, nevertheless, were laboring under the burdens imposed upon them by the liquor-traffic. Just as an entire army, though largely composed of brave men, may be beaten into a hopeless rout if a few score in its line of battle awaiting a charge puts up the despairing cry of "*Sauve qui peut!*" so the best material for citizenship may find progress blocked, if, in addition to surmounting obstacles itself, it is obliged to drag useless lumber with it. The chief evil of the liquor-traffic is that, as the rain falls alike upon the just and unjust, so it imposes its multiform burdens upon an entire community, permitting nothing in the wide range of its diversified interests to escape. The sober, the industrious, the thrifty citizen bears his portion, if in a

Neil Dow, *The Reminiscences of Neil Dow* (Portland, Me.: 1898), pp. 176-78, 204-8, 220, 275-76, 284, 331-32.

manner less apparent than do those through whose indiscretions the more palpable injury is wrought.

Good authorities upon such matters have held that it is a dangerous, generally a disastrous, strain to put upon the courage and discipline of the best troops to expose them to a fire which would put one in ten of their number *hors du combat*. In such cases the repulse to be expected would not be due alone to the direct loss sustained by the decimation; more than that would be subtracted in one way or another from the fighting force of the unscathed nine. So the citizens of Maine were exposed to and suffered from the rifle-pits and batteries of a trade, for years intrenched in the fallacy, fostered by the law which made them quasi-representatives of the state, that they served a useful purpose.

True, therefore, as it is that in her early days Maine suffered from the trade to which at length the intelligence, virtue, conscience and patriotism of her people denied legal foothold within her borders, that great moral awakening, that marvelous political revolution, that long stride in legislation in which the state recognized its right and asserted its determination to be freed from the moral and material incubus of the rum trade, testify in themselves volumes to the possession by the masses of her people of all those elements which must underlie a prosperous and progressive nation. Honest, industrious, frugal, enterprising, thoughtful, they were themselves on the highway to prosperity, and were making plain the paths to plenty for all who should profit by their example and be guided by their precepts. When at length they found their way onward blocked by a trade serving no useful purpose whatever, they devoted themselves to removing the enemy obstructing their progress.

Believing, as I devoutly do, that Maine could not be to-day what she is, rich in all that goes to make for the substantial prosperity and true happiness of a virtuous people, but for the bulwark she erected in Prohibition years ago to protect herself from the injury and demoralization of the liquor-traffic, I yet recognize with pride the high average of her early inhabitants in all excellent qualities. Had the men of Maine been less then than what they were, it would have been left to some other state, possessing those virtues which, happily, they did not lack, to have led the way, as did Maine, in the most difficult, unpopular and important moral revolution of their time.

In 1850 not a savings bank existed in Maine. By the census of 1890, although ranking as the twenty-ninth among her sisters in the Union in point of population, only five outrank her in the number of her depositors, and only six in the total amount of deposits. By that census, New Jersey, with a population of 1,444,933, had 117,853 depositors in those institutions, and Ohio, with 3,672,310 people, had 73,335, while Maine, with less than half the population of the former and less than a fifth of the latter, had 132,192 depositors. Other comparisons might be instituted, all indicating the general prosperity of the state, but it is not necessary. . . .

• • •

. . . I do not remember any period of my life, after I was of sufficient age to observe and to think for myself, when the awful effects of intemperance did not claim from me more than merely casual thought. In my early youth a near neighbor was a confirmed inebriate. Because of his habits, he and his unfortunate family, from time to time, required aid from my parents. His case, therefore, served at our table and fireside to add weight to the precepts of sobriety and abstinence, ordinarily inculcated in New England Quaker homes of the period. It required no unusual mental power in me, even as a small lad, to trace to drink the comparative wretchedness and squalor in that drunken neighbor's home.

When a small boy, I was much impressed by hearing my father say at the dinner-table that he had that forenoon witnessed the conveyance of a tract of land, now in the business portion of Portland, occupied by stores. It was transferred to settle a score, charged at the shop of the grantee against the grantor, for liquor furnished in the glass and drunk on the premises. The incident was indelibly fixed in my memory by the remark with which my father opened the topic: "At last poor Friend ——— has drunk up his land!" This expression arrested my youthful attention sufficiently to enable me to comprehend something of the conversation which followed.

My mother was an exceedingly kind and charitable woman. No worthy applicant for aid was turned empty-handed from her door. She made it a duty to investigate the case of every applicant, where she was not previously informed, and I was frequently her companion in the errands with which she thus charged herself, seeing for myself much that led her to pour precept after precept into my willing ears. By her I was taught to abhor the very idea of liquor drinking, and at her feet, not less from her example than from her precept, I came to believe that to be indifferent to the welfare of others was a sin and a shame. As I grew older, therefore, I was prepared to observe, perhaps at an earlier age than is the case with many, the devastating effects of intemperance.

In my younger manhood, before I reached my majority, my attention was called to the subject as a matter of practical importance. I was brought into contact with many who depended upon daily manual labor for support, and to whom, therefore, health, strength, and continuous employment were all-important. My interest in them was easily enlisted, and I came to know something, through my opportunities for close personal observation, of the condition of their families. I was impressed, not only with the prevalence of drunkenness among them, which indeed was more or less apparent in all classes of society, but by the evident inability of workmen to provide for the pressing necessities of their families when spending so much as was their habit for intoxicants.

I saw health impaired, capacity undermined, employment lost. I saw wives and children suffering from the drinking habits of husbands and fathers long before the latter could be said to have become drunkards, in the parlance of that day. I saw that, as a rule, neither industry, thrift, prudence, saving nor comfort was to be found where indulgence in intoxicants prevailed. Called often to render assistance in these cases, my indignation at the men who brought so much suffering upon their families for the gratification, as it then seemed to me, of a mere taste for liquor, softened into pity and sympathy when I found them the apparently helpless victims of a controlling appetite that was dragging them to ruin. My observation of this had its effect in determining the position I afterwards took.

I had attended meetings held under the auspices of those who traced their interest to the influence of the "Sixty-Niners," * and I was quite prepared to take a stand when called upon to do so. The opportunity soon offered. I was 24 years of age at the time. The Deluge

* A temperance group, composed of 69 members, organized in Portland, Maine.

Engine-company, of which I was clerk, was about to celebrate its first anniversary. It was proposed that the officers be directed to provide liquors for the occasion at the company's expense. I took the floor and opposed the proposition as earnestly as I could. There was considerable discussion, and some feeling was developed, but I was sustained by the company. This was due, I think, quite as much to the personal regard of the members for me (I was the junior of most of them) as to their full assent to my views.

That speech caused some talk outside the company, and a short time thereafter I was called upon to speak at a temperance meeting where I had expected to be a listener. Soon I was invited to be one of the announced speakers at a meeting to be held, and prepared for the occasion to the extent of writing out in full what I proposed to say.

In the winter of 1815, the Maine Charitable Mechanics' Association was organized in Portland. I became a member of it almost immediately after my majority. That society yet exists, after a long life of varied prosperity. In its earlier days, especially, it exerted great influence in the town, and soon came to be a potential agency in the propagation of the principles underlying the temperance reform.

Its members had unusual opportunities to see the evil effects of the liquor-traffic and the drinking habits of the day. Through them most of the laboring men of the town found employment. They paid out a large portion of the money distributed as wages for skilled, as well as unskilled, labor, and they had constantly before them the evidence that no inconsiderable proportion was expended for liquor. They saw, too, in the resulting indisposition to work, in the loss of time from drinking, and the impairment of energy, capacity and health by debauch that the money thus spent was more unwisely used than if thrown into the sea.

In those days, master-mechanics were brought into contact with the families of their employees much more than now. They saw the poverty, misery and disease brought upon wives and children by the excess in drink of the husband and father, and their sympathies were aroused. They were practical men of affairs. They knew that their own success depended in great measure upon the capacity, skill and faithfulness of their employees but they were often compelled to pay for untrustworthiness and incapacity caused by drink where they had contracted for better service. They knew, too, that their own prosperity, and that of the town in which they lived, were interchangeable, and they were in a condition to be easily convinced that the public weal could be served by sober and industrious, but never by drunken and shiftless citizens. It is not strange, therefore, that the Mechanics' Association came to consider ways and means of mitigating the terrible evils of intemperance.

• • •

Many times, prompted thereto by the seeming indifference and sometimes strenuous opposition of those whom I knew to be good citizens, and whom I believed desired to be consistent Christians, I have considered anew that decision, and have asked myself if the object sought was worthy the sacrifices it necessitated. But such reconsiderations have served to confirm me, if possible, more strongly than before in the belief that nothing is more productive of wretchedness for the individual, or more obstructive to the general progress and prosperity of the state, than the traffic in intoxicating drinks, and never, from the day of my early determination, have I doubted that duty demanded of me unrelenting and uncompromising opposition to that trade.

• • •

Much of modern antagonism to Prohibition covers its real purpose —support of the liquor-traffic—by parading professions of great confidence in what it terms "moral influences," and not infrequently cites the Washingtonian reformation by way of illustration. Yet that reform was a most effective agency in securing anti-liquor-selling legislation in Maine. In the city of Portland alone, within a year of its organization, that society numbered 1,225, of whom it was estimated at the time that at least 1,000 had, before taking the Pledge, diverted of their small, hard-earned wages, on an average, about twelve cents a day from the support of their families to provide themselves with drink. That aggregated a considerable sum for so small a city as Portland then was to expend for that which served no useful purpose, and which reduced to a large, if not exactly ascertainable per cent, the earning capacity of those who purchased it. The effect of stopping this leakage from the pockets of the working-men into the tills of the liquor-seller resulted in an increase of the receipts of dealers in family supplies larger than was the reduction of the sums paid for liquor; this was because with the abandonment of drink the working-men could earn more money, which, added to that no longer expended for rum, was available for the comports of life.

The friends of temperance were not backward in using these facts to show that the less the sale of liquor the greater the prosperity of the community, and to argue if there were no liquor-shops every legitimate business would be improved. The step, therefore, was easy, natural, and logical toward condemnation of the liquor trade by law. Right here the friends of the Washingtonian movement were confronted by the same kind of charges, concocted by the liquor-dealers, so commonly in later days applied to Prohibition. Here are some of them: "The Washingtonian movement does no good." "Just as much liquor is drunk now as ever." "More rum is sold now than formerly." "These fellows (pledged Washingtonians) may not drink as publicly as before, but they keep their supplies at home, drink in private, and consume more than ever."

• • •

Many, if not most, of these abodes of misery were in the vicinage of places where liquor was sold. That was to be expected. Just as the smoke issuing from the chimney of a factory settles upon and to an extent blackens everything in the neighborhood, so, though the emanations from these moral pest-houses were to be traced far and near, they were generally more dense, if not blacker, in their immediate proximity. Hence those engaged in this work of charitable investigation were observed and known to those whose frightful trade made charity necessary.

Efforts in this direction were obnoxious to the vendors of intoxicants. By intuition they foresaw that such investigation would expose the nature of the business in which they were engaged, and they knew enough of human nature to understand that those with hearts sufficiently warm to be touched by the misery thus disclosed must be led to abhor the trade of which that wretchedness was the product. Perhaps, too, they feared that some with wills strong enough might be led to invoke law as a protection from such sin and shame and crime as their business was pouring out in an ever-widening stream to befoul what otherwise might be virtue, plenty, happiness, and peace in the community.

• • •

To return to the matter of my election as mayor, I was inaugurated on the twenty-fourth of April, 1851, and my address, which covered as well the topics ordinarily treated in such papers, after referring to the supposed necessity for a new almshouse and house of correction, contained the following:

> In my opinion the present almshouse is sufficiently spacious and may be rendered comfortable and well arranged, at a very small expense, for the decent and proper maintenance of all those who would be thrown upon the city for support, but for the illegal traffic in intoxicating drinks.
>
> I call your attention to this latter subject, as one of deep importance to the city, in every point of view. The illegal traffic in intoxicating drinks is an evil of frightful magnitude, and has been rapidly increasing among us within the two or three years past. The inevitable tendency of this traffic is to impoverish and degrade the people; to convert sober men and good citizens into drunkards and bad members of society; to corrupt the young and inexperienced—and to render many families wretched as well as poor—which but for this business, would be prosperous and happy. Our almshouses, our jails, hospitals, lunatic asylums, and our prisons are filled with the miserable victims of this odious traffic, which is the fruitful parent of every species of misery, vice and crime, in every degree of intensity—while it has no redeeming feature; it carries poverty, pauperism, degradation, crime, and death to thousands, while it benefits nobody.
>
> There is no fact better established than this, that the traffic in intoxicating drinks tends more to the degradation and impoverishment of the people than all other causes of evil combined; its existence is incompatible with the general welfare and prosperity of the community. All classes of society have the deepest interest in its suppression. As a question of domestic and political economy, of earnings and savings, of annual accumulating wealth to the city, this subject demands the highest consideration. I have good reason to believe that a very large majority of the people of this city and of the state, are in favor of the adoption of some

effectual measures for the suppression of a business which is at war with every principle of humanity and enlightened patriotism, and which violates the law of God as well as the law of the land.

I have only to add, that any measure you may think it proper to adopt, tending to restrain or to suppress this traffic, shall have my cordial co-operation. This subject is now exciting the attention of the people of all the states of the Union; and it has been considered so important by the people of Ohio and Michigan, that a provision has been inserted in the recently revised constitutions of those states, depriving their legislatures of the power of enacting any law to grant licenses for the sale of intoxicating drinks, and providing that such liquors shall only be sold for medicinal and mechanical purposes.

In the larger towns and cities in this state, no decisive movement can be made to suppress the numerous drinking houses and tippling shops by which they are infested without the enactment of a law for that purpose which shall be sufficiently stringent in its provisions and summary in its processes to effect its objects. I commend this subject to your attention, as one eminently worthy your regard.

part five

THEODORE WELD: DIVINE INTENT AND HUMAN INADEQUACY

All of the reformers discussed previously assumed that God directed them to engage in reform activities. Garrison and Parker's confidence that they understood God's will and spoke for Him, Beecher's conviction that God intended His clergy to set a moral standard for society, and Dow's belief that he, as interpreter of God's will, had a right to make laws restricting men's actions, were all examples of reformers who acted with the assurance that came from belief in God direction. Theodore Weld also believed in God direction, but Weld's reform activities were hampered by his doubts as to exactly what God intended man to do. Weld was a devout reformer and, as his letters make so clear, a devout Christian. But translating Christian devotion into social programs was Weld's problem. Weld was convinced slavery was immoral, but seeking the proper means to an end carried him to positions of which he was unsure. Weld's seeking is both explicit and implicit in many of his letters, while his confidence that slavery was immoral is clear in his anti-slavery tract, *The Bible Against Slavery*.

source **12**

The Bible Against Slavery

Theodore Weld

We proceed to state affirmatively that, ENSLAVING MEN IS REDUCING THEM TO ARTICLES OF PROPERTY—making free agents, chattels—converting persons, into things—sinking immortality, into merchandize. A slave is one held in this condition. "In law he owns nothing, and can acquire nothing." His right to himself is abrogated. If he say my hands, my feet, my body, my mind, myself, they are figures of speech. To use himself for his own good, is a CRIME. To keep what he earns, is stealing. To take his body into his own keeping, is insurrection. In a word, the profit of his master is made the END of his being and he a mere means to that end—a mere means to an end into which his interests do not enter, of which they constitute no portion.[1] MAN, sunk to a thing! the intrinsic element, the principle of slavery; MEN, bartered, leased, mortgaged, bequeathed, invoiced, shipped in cargoes, stored as goods, taken on executions, and knocked off at public outcry!

Theodore Weld, *The Bible Against Slavery* (New York, 1835), pp. 7-15.

[1] Whatever system sinks man from an END to a mere means, just so far makes him a slave. Hence West India apprenticeship retains the cardinal principle of slavery. The apprentice, during three-fourths of his time, is still forced to labor, and robbed of his earnings; just so far forth he is a mere means, a slave. True, in other respects slavery is abolished in the British West Indies. Its bloodiest features are blotted out—but the meanest and most despicable of all—forcing the poor to work for the rich without pay three-fourths of their time, with a legal officer to flog them if they demur at the outrage, is one of the provisions of the "Emancipation Act"! For the glories of that luminary, abolitionists thank God, while they mourn that it rose behind clouds, and shines through an eclipse.

Their rights, another's conveniences; their interests, wares on sale; their happiness, a household utensil; their personal inalienable ownership, a serviceable article, or a plaything, as best suits the humor of the hour; their deathless nature, conscience, social affections, sympathies, hopes—marketable commodities! We repeat it, the reduction of persons to things; not robbing a man of privileges, but of himself; not loading with burdens, but making him a beast of burden; not restraining liberty, but subverting it; not curtailing rights, but abolishing them; not inflicting personal cruelty, but annihilating personality; not exacting involuntary labor, but sinking him into an implement of labor; not abridging human comforts, but abrogating human nature; not depriving an animal of immunities, but despoiling a rational being of attributes—uncreating a MAN, to make room for a thing!

That this is American slavery, is shown by the laws of slave states. Judge Stroud, in his "Sketch of the Laws relating to Slavery," says, "The cardinal principle of slavery, that the slave is not to be ranked among sentient beings, but among things—obtains as undoubted law in all of these [the slave] states." The law of South Carolina thus lays down the principle, "Slaves shall be deemed, held, taken, reputed, and adjudged in law to be chattels personal in the hands of their owners and possessors, and their executors, administrators, and assigns, to ALL INTENTS, CONSTRUCTIONS, AND PURPOSES WHATSOEVER."—Brevard's Digest, 229. In Louisiana, "A slave is one who is in the power of a master to whom he belongs; the master may sell him, dispose of his person, his industry, and his labor; he can do nothing, possess nothing, nor acquire any thing, but what must belong to his master. —Civ. Code of Louisiana, Art. 35.

This is American slavery. The eternal distinction between a person and a thing, trampled underfoot—the crowning distinction of all others —alike the source, the test, and the measure of their value—the rational, immortal principle, consecrated by God to universal homage, in a baptism of glory and honor by the gift of His Son, His Spirit, His word, His presence, providence, and power; His shield, and staff, and sheltering wing; His opening heavens, and angels ministering, and chariots of fire, and songs of morning stars, and a great voice in heaven, proclaiming eternal sanctions, and confirming the word with signs following.

Having stated the principle of American slavery, we ask, DOES THE BIBLE SANCTION SUCH A PRINCIPLE?[2] "To the law and the testimony?" First, the moral law. Just after the Israelites were emancipated from their bondage in Egypt, while they stood before Sinai to receive the law, as the trumpet waxed louder, and mount quaked and blazed, God spake the ten commandments from the midst of clouds and thunderings. Two of those commandments deal death to slavery. "THOU SHALT NOT STEAL," or, "thou shalt not take from another what belongs to him." All man's powers are God's gift to him. That they are his own, is proved from the fact that God has given them to him alone—that each of them is a part of himself, and all of them together constitute himself. All else that belongs to man is acquired by the use of these powers. The interest belongs to him, because the principal does; the product is his, because he is the producer. Ownership of anything, is ownership of its use. The right to use according to will, is itself ownership. The eighth commandment presupposes and assumes the right of every man to his powers, and their product. Slavery robs of both. A man's right to himself, is the only right absolutely original and intrinsic—his right to whatever else that belongs to him is merely relative to this, is derived from it, and held only by virtue of it. SELF-RIGHT is the foundation right—the post in the middle, to which all other rights are fastened. Slaveholders, when talking about their RIGHT to their slaves, always assume their own right to themselves. What slaveholder ever undertook to prove his right to himself? He knows it to be a self-evident proposition, that a man belongs to himself—that the right is intrinsic and absolute. In making out his own title, he makes out the title of every human being. As the fact of being a man is itself the title, the whole human family have one common title deed. If one man's title is valid, all are valid. If one is worthless, all are. To deny the validity of the SLAVE's title is to deny the validity of

[2] The Bible record of actions is no comment on their moral character. It vouches for them as facts, not as virtues. It records without rebuke, Noah's drunkenness, Lot's incest, and the lies of Jacob and his mother—not only single acts, but usages, such as polygamy and concubinage, are entered on the record without censure. Is that silent entry God's endorsement? Because the Bible in its catalogue of human actions, does not stamp on every crime its name and number, and write against it, this is a crime—does that wash out its guilt, and bleach into a virtue?

HIS OWN; and yet in the act of making a man a slave, the slaveholder ASSERTS the validity of his own title, while he seizes him as his property who has the same title. Further, in making him a slave, he does not merely disfranchise the humanity of one individual, but of UNIVERSAL MAN. He destroys the foundations. He annihilates all rights. He attacks not only the human race, but universal being, and rushes upon JEHOVAH. For rights are rights. God's are no more—man's are no less.

The eighth commandment forbids the taking of any part of that which belongs to another. Slavery takes the whole. Does the same Bible which prohibits the taking of anything from him, sanction the taking of everything? Does it thunder wrath against him who robs his neighbor of a cent, yet bid God speed to him who robs his neighbor of himself? Slaveholding is the highest possible violation of the eighth commandment. To take from a man his earnings, is theft. But to take the earner, is a compound, life-long theft—supreme robbery, that vaults up the climax at a leap—the dread, terrific, giant robbery, that towers among other robberies a solitary horror, monarch of the realm. The eighth commandment forbids the taking away, and the tenth adds, "THOU SHALT NOT COVET ANYTHING THAT IS THY NEIGHBOR'S," thus guarding every man's right to himself and his property, by making not only the actual taking away a sin, but even that state of mind which would tempt to it. Who ever made human beings slaves, without coveting them? Why take from them their time, labor, liberty, right of self-preservation and improvement, their right to acquire property, to worship according to conscience, to search the Scriptures, to live with their families, and their right to their own bodies, if they do not desire them? They COVET them for purposes of gain, convenience, lust of dominion, of sensual gratification, of pride and ostentation. THEY BREAK THE TENTH COMMANDMENT, and pluck down upon their heads the plagues that are written in the book—Ten commandments constitute the brief compend of human duty—Two of these brand slavery as sin.

If God permitted man to hold man as property, why did he punish for stealing that kind of property infinitely more than for stealing any other kind of property? Why did he punish with death for stealing a very little of that sort of property, and make a mere fine, the penalty for stealing a thousand times as much, of any other sort of property—especially if God did by his own act annihilate the difference between man and property, by putting him on a level with it?

The atrociousness of a crime depends much upon the nature, character, and condition of the victim. To steal is a crime, whoever the thief, or whatever the plunder. To steal bread from a full man, is theft: to steal it from a starving man, is both theft and murder. If I steal my neighbor's property, the crime consists not in altering the nature of the article, but in shifting its relation from him to me. But when I take my neighbor himself, and first make him property, and then my property, the latter act, which was the sole crime in the former case, dwindles to nothing. The sin in stealing a man, is not the transfer from its owner to another of that which is already property, but the turning of personality into property. True, the attributes of man remain, but the rights and immunities which grow out of them are annihilated. It is the just law both of persons and revelation to regard things and beings as they are; and the sum of religion, to feel and act toward them according to their value. Knowingly to treat them otherwise is sin; and the degree of violence done to their nature, relations, and value, measures its guilt. When things are sundered which God has indissolubly joined, or confounded in one, which he has separated by infinite extremes; when sacred and eternal distinctions, which he has garnished with glory, are derided and set at nought, then, if ever, sin reddens to its "scarlet dye." The sin specified in the passage, is that of doing violence to the nature of a man—to his intrinsic value as a rational being, and blotting out the exalted distinction stamped upon him by his Maker. In the verse preceding, and in that which follows, the same principle is laid down. Verse 15: "He that smiteth his father or his mother shall surely be put to death." Verse 17: "He that curseth his father or his mother, shall surely be put to death." If a Jew smote his neighbor, the law merely smote him in return; but if the blow was given to a parent, it struck the smiter dead. The parental relation is the centre of human society. God guards it with peculiar care. To violate that, is to violate all. Whoever trampled on that, showed that no relation had any sacredness in his eyes—that he was unfit to move among human relations who had violated one so sacred and tender. Therefore, the Mosaic law uplifted his bleeding corpse, and brandished the ghastly terror around the parental relation to guard it from impious inroads.

Why such a difference in penalties, for the same act? Answer.

(1) The relation violated was obvious—the distinction between parents and others manifest, dictated by natural affection—a law of the constitution. (2) The act was violence to nature—a suicide on constitutional susceptibilities. (3) The parental relationship, then as now, was the focal point of the social system, and required powerful safeguards. "Honor thy father and thy mother" stands at the head of those commands which prescribe the duties of man to man; and, throughout the Bible, the parental state is God's favorite illustration of his own relations to the whole human family. In this case death was to be inflicted not for smiting a man, but a parent—a distinction cherished by God, and around which, He threw up a bulwark of defence. In the next verse, "He that stealeth a man, . . ." the SAME PRINCIPLE is wrought out in still stronger relief. The crime to be punished with death was not the taking of property from its owner, but the doing violence to an immortal nature, blotting out a sacred distinction, making MEN "chattels." The incessant pains taken in the Old Testament to separate human beings from brutes and things, shows God's regard for his own distinction.

"In the beginning" it was uttered in heaven, and proclaimed to the universe as it rose into being. Creation was arrayed at the instant of its birth, to do it homage. It paused in adoration while God ushered forth its crowning work. Why that dread pause and that creating arm held back in mid-career and that high conference in the godhead? "Let us make man in OUR IMAGE after OUR LIKENESS, AND LET HIM HAVE DOMINION over the fish of the sea, and over the fowl of the air, and over the cattle, and over all the earth." Then while every living thing, with land, and sea, and firmament, and marshalled worlds, waited to swell the shout of morning stare—then "GOD CREATED MAN IN HIS OWN IMAGE; IN THE IMAGE OF GOD CREATED HE HIM." This solves the problem, IN THE IMAGE OF GOD, CREATED HE HIM. Well might the sons of God shout, "Amen."

source 13

From *The Letters*

Theodore Weld

TO MR. T. D. WELD *

DEAR SIR:

You have been appointed an Agent of the American Anti-Slavery Society; and will receive the following instructions from the Executive Committee, as a brief expression of the principles they wish you to inculcate, and the course of conduct they wish you to pursue in this agency.

The general principles of the Society are set forth in the Declaration, signed by the members of the Convention which formed it at Philadelphia, Dec. 7, 1833. Our object is, the overthrow of American slavery, the most atrocious and oppressive system of bondage that has ever existed in any country. We expect to accomplish this, mainly by showing to the public its true character and legitimate fruits, its contrariety to the first principles of religion, morals, and humanity, and its special inconsistency with our pretensions, as a free, humane, and enlightened people. In this way, by the force of truth, we expect to correct the common errors that prevail respecting slavery, and to produce a just public sentiment, which shall appeal both to the conscience and love of character, of our slave-holding fellow-citizens, and convince

Gilbert H. Barnes and Dwight L. Dumond, eds., *The Letters of Theodore Dwight Weld, Angelina Grimké Weld and Sarah Grimké* (New York: American Historical Association, 1934), I, 125-28, 247-48, 491-92, 506-7; II, 535, 880-81, 888-89, 894.

* Weld followed these instructions, accepting fully the principle that the abolitionist should stick to preaching the sin of slavery and not propose plans to abolish it. The instructions then reflected Weld's own views.

them that both their duty and their welfare require the immediate abolition of slavery.

You will inculcate every where, the great fundamental principle of IMMEDIATE ABOLITION, as the duty of all masters, on the ground that slavery is both unjust and unprofitable. Insist principally on the SIN OF SLAVERY, because our main hope is in the consciences of men, and it requires little logic to prove that it is always safe to do right. To question this, is to impeach the superintending Providence of God.

We reprobate the idea of compensation to slave holders, because it implies the right of slavery. It is also unnecessary, because the abolition of slavery will be an advantage, as free labor is found to be more profitable than the labor of slaves. We also reprobate all plans of expatriation, by whatever specious pretences covered, as a remedy for slavery, for they all proceed from prejudice against color; and we hold that the duty of the whites in regard to this cruel prejudice is not to indulge it, but to repent and overcome it.

The people of color ought at once to be emancipated and recognized as citizens, and their rights secured as such, equal in all respects to others, according to the cardinal principle laid down in the American Declaration of Independence. Of course we have nothing to do with any *equal* laws which the states may make, to prevent or punish vagrancy, idleness, and crime, either in whites or blacks.

Do not allow yourself to be drawn away from the main object, to exhibit a detailed PLAN of abolition; for men's consciences will be greatly relieved from the feeling of present duty, by any objections or difficulties which they can find or fancy in your plan. Let the *principle* be decided on, of immediate abolition, and the plans will easily present themselves. What ought to be done can be done. If the *great* question were decided, and if half the ingenuity now employed to defend slavery were employed to abolish it, it would impeach the wisdom of American statesmen to say they could not, with the Divine blessing, steer the ship through.

You will make yourself familiar with FACTS, for they chiefly influence reflecting minds. Be careful to use only facts that are well authenticated, and always state them with the precision of a witness under oath. You cannot do our cause a greater injury than by overstating facts. Clarkson's "Thoughts," and Stuart's "West India Question," are Magazines of facts respecting the safety and benefit of immediate emancipation. Mrs. Child's Book, Stroud's Slave Laws, Paxton's and Rankin's Letters, D. L. Child's Address, are good authorities respecting the character of American slavery. The African Repository and Garrison's Thoughts will show the whole subject of expatriation.

The field marked out by the Committee for your agency is the State of Ohio.

The Committee expect you to confine your labors to that field, unless some special circumstances call you elsewhere. And in such case you will confer with the Committee before changing your field, if time will allow. And if not, we wish immediate notice of the fact.

In traversing your field, you will generally find it wise to visit first several prominent places in it, particularly those where it is known our cause has friends. In going to a place, you will naturally call upon those who are friendly to our objects, and take advice from them. Also call on ministers of the gospel and other leading characters, and labor specially to enlighten them and secure their favor and influence. Ministers are the hinges of community, and ought to be moved, if possible. If they can be gained, much is gained. But if not, you will not be discouraged; and if not plainly inexpedient, attempt to obtain a house of worship; or if none can be had, some other convenient place—and hold a public meeting, where you can present our cause, its facts, arguments and appeals, to as many people as you can collect, by notices in pulpits and newspapers, and other proper means.

Form Auxiliary Societies, both male and female, in every place where it is practicable. Even if such societies are very small at the outset, they may do much good as centres of light, and means of future access to the people. Encourage them to raise funds and apply them in purchasing and circulating anti-slavery publications gratuitously; particularly the *Anti-Slavery Reporter,* of which you will keep specimens with you, and which can always be had of the Society at $2.00 per 100. You are at liberty, with due discretion, to recommend other publications, *so far* as they advocate our views of immediate abolition. We hold ourselves responsible only for our own.

You are not to take up collections in your public meetings, as the practice often prevents persons from attending, whom it might be desirable to reach. Let this be stated in the public notice of the meeting. If you find individuals friendly to our views, who are able to give us money, you will make special personal application, and urge upon them the duty of liberally supporting this cause. You can also give notice of some place where those disposed can give you their donations. Generally, it is best to invite them to do this *the next morning*.

We shall expect you to write frequently to the Secretary for Domestic Correspondence, and give minute accounts of your proceedings and success. If you receive money for the Society, you will transmit it, *by mail,* WITHOUT DELAY, to the Treasurer.

Always keep us advised, if possible, of the place where letters may reach you.

Believing as we do, that the hearts of all men are in the hand of Almighty God, we wish particularly to engage the prayers of all good men in behalf of our enterprise. Let them pray that *we* and our agents may have Divine guidance and zeal; and slave-holders, penitence; and slaves, patience; and statesmen, wisdom; so that this grand experiment of moral influence may be crowned with glorious and speedy success. Especially stir up ministers and others to the duty of making continual mention of the oppressed slaves in all social and public prayers. And as far as you can, procure the stated observance of the LAST MONDAY EVENING in every month, as a season of special prayer in behalf of the people of color.

We will only remind you, that the Society is but the almoner of the public—that the silver and the gold are the Lord's—that the amount as yet set apart by his people for promoting this particular object is small—our work is great and our resources limited—and we therefore trust that you will not fail to use a faithful economy in regard to the expenses of traveling, and reduce them as low as you can without impairing your usefulness.

Anti-Slavery Office
New York, Feb. 20, 1834

WELD TO LEWIS TAPPAN

Pittsburgh, Pa., Dec. 22, 1835 *

MY DEAR BROTHER TAPPAN:

I have this moment read your letter.

The terrors of God! The faintest gleam of them smites men with trembling or maddens with frenzy. Oh then whose heart can endure, whose hands be strong when the breath of God sets the Universe on fire and a million worlds burn down at once! My brother I can't resist the conviction that this terrible rebuke is but a single herald sent in advance to announce the coming of a host. The Land is full of blood. It will [mutilated] cover the slain. The groans of slaughtered thousands go up to heaven from the dust where they welter. Truth has fallen in the streets. Judgment is turned away backward. Warnings have been unheeded. Entreaties and tears have been scoffed at. The poor have cried and ears have been stopped and hearts have been steeled; and avarice has clutched the last pittance, and lust has gorged itself with spoil, and prejudice has spurned God's image with loathing, and passion has rushed upon the helpless and trodden down the needy in the gates; and when iniquity has been visited by terrible rebuke, it has swelled with pride and gnashed with rage, and cursed the poor and blasphemed God—scorning repentance and defying wrath to the uttermost. Shall I not visit for these things and shall not my soul be avenged on a nation like this? What can save us as a nation but repentance—immediate, profound, *public,* proclaimed abroad, wide as our infamy and damning guilt have gone!

Works meet for repentance too, everywhere before the sun. The *breaking off* by righteousness and turning to the Lord, not merely the ashes and sackcloth and sitting in dust, with dishevelled hair and streaming tears and lamentation and wailing, *but* confession—yea on the house tops—and *restoration* to the uttermost tho' it bring to beggary, and loosing the bonds, undoing the burdens, breaking every yoke, dealing bread to the hungry, hiring the poor that are cast out, and

* The year 1835 was a year marked by frequent incidents of violence directed against abolitionists. In this letter we see Weld's conviction that the millennium is about to come and with it the destruction of mankind. They, the reformers, must awaken society to the danger. Here we see Weld confident that the last demon will be cast out. That confidence was soon to waiver.

satisfying the afflicted *soul.* This may save us. God grant it may not be too late!! I have run on and on almost incoherently perchance, but this awful calamity which has whelmed the queen-city of the Land seems to me so like Jehovah's voice, its last warning spoken in articulate thunder over the sealed ear of a besotted people drugged by its sins into the sleep of death, that my forebodings have all rushed out *en masse.* God be praised that your firm have not lost *all.* It was so reported here last night. You must be greatly cramped in your operations for a while at least. Well the rest of us will work the harder and do the more. God be thanked we have a heart to it, and will swing higher and strike deeper than ever. If the money and the presses are all burned up then God will multiply *men* and the living voice shall ring in every corner and on every hill till the last demon is cast out. . . .

WELD TO SARAH AND ANGELINA GRIMKÉ

Dec. 15, 1837 *

My dear sister are you in earnest when you express horror at the awful sin of taking human life? You think Lovejoy committed murder. Why? Because he thought it was "no matter how soon" Bishop's life was "worn out." Human life is human life; and it is a real violation of the sixth commandment to violate the laws of its organization in *one* case as *another;* and just as real a violation of the *principle* to violate *some* of *these gradually,* as to violate them *all, all at once;* or in other words to *kill* outright. Here is the *cord of life.* To *cut it short off,* if done to another, is *murder;* to one's self, suicide; but suppose instead of cutting *it* off, you cut off one of its *strands,* a very *small* one, if you please; or suppose, instead of *cutting* the cord at all you *untwist it;* thus instead of shortening its *length* you weaken its *strength.* Each and all of these acts are violations of the *same great principle,* that principle which God set the sixth commandment to guard. Some almost make a *virtue*—I had like to have said a *Savior*—of wearing out as *soon as they can,* or in other words of *violating God's laws* promulg[at]ed thro *their own organization,* as fast and as far as possible, if they only are doing good in some way. So a man may rob on the highway, "no matter how soon" or how much, if he uses all the money in relieving the poor, printing

* Here Weld argues for the doctrine of nonviolence.

[B]ibles, anti-slavery tracts, etc.; and if he should rob the rich so constantly and with such incessant vigor out of zeal to help the poor and save the oppressed, that he should "wear out" and be "confirmed in the conviction" that it was "no matter how soon," would that help the matter? He "wears out"—a *robber*. True a very *benevolent* one—but a robber. Oh but you will say, I don't deliberately *design* to violate the laws of my *organization*. *Granted*. So the doctor who drives down Broadway full gallop in benevolent haste to see a patient, don't [*sic*] *design* to run over women and children, but run over them he does at every crossing, and kills a score before he gets to his patient. The doctor is bound *deliberately* to *design* NOT to run over them and to manage his horse *accordingly*. And you and I and everybody are bo[u]nd deliberately to *design* NOT to violate the laws of our organization, and to *manage ourselves accordingly,* as a most solemn duty. Why did God give us bodies with a machinery made on *purpose* to run 70 or 80 years—constructed on that very principle—and set this machinery up here, in *this world?* I answer, in order that we might *keep it running* 70 or 80 years *here* and do as much good as we can with it *all the time,* without *violating the laws* that *regulate* its running, and thus impiously *stop it before the time* by violence inflicted on it and on its holy author, contempt poured and insult and defiance added. I write in deep and solemn earnest on this matter my beloved sisters, for my own sins in this respect rise up before me in crimsoned crowds and shriek their warning in my ears and bid me shriek them in the ears of others till they tingle. I have sinned with a high hand and I trust God has granted me *repentance* unto *life* even in this world (for I feel new health every day). And now my daily prayer is touching this matter, "deliver me from *blood guiltiness* oh God, thou God of *my* salvation." And that I do not separate prayer and *works, ye* are my witnesses and so is this sheet. . . .

WELD TO ANGELINA AND SARAH GRIMKÉ

Dec. 28, 1837

Now my dear sisters, I have said nothing about it because at a time like this when an accumulation of superficial plausibilities in the place of argument and investigation are ruining [?] the church, I will not consent to meet plausibilities *by* mere plausibilities; and to *settle* the government question would require more than the flippancies that might be thrown off in a *letter,* or in a little hurried conversation. But the chief reason is that the "government question" can be settled only by settling a *previous* question which has not been yet touched or to my knowledge hinted at in this controversy, and that is the true ground of God's right to govern. The nature of Government, its *scope,* its *legitimacy,* its righteousness, all turn upon that pivot. I could not bear to touch the subject without going into an argument and range [?] of induction for which I had the time; and I long ago made up my mind that the throwing out of opinions on subjects *vital to human well-being* without a development of the *grounds* of those opinions, showing them to be *immutable truth,* was smiting the world with a curse—a curse that for ages has downed every green thing before it. Another reason why I have not lisped a syllable in any of my letters about "Peace" is that without previously discussing another point, whatever I might say would almost inevitably produce an impression on your minds which would lead to a conclusion that I did not design. You would be almost certain to misconstrue my meaning because the light of the *previous* question is indispensible as a medium thro which to look at *this.*

Now this may all be owing to my shallowness or ignorance or pride of opinion or wrongheadedness. If so, I know you will pity and pray for me and try to enlighten me, and God will assuredly grant me repentance to the acknowledgment of the truth, if I have a heart [?] to receive the gift. Now all this instead of satisfying you my sisters will only grieve you the more, I doubt not; and [I] am sorry for it, but really cannot help it. What a world of enigmas, anomalies, solecisms, and contradictory whims is that mysterious riddle, the human mind. I used to find it an exceedingly sore trial to my patience when I came in contact with a mind entertaining opinions which seemed to me utterly absurd, as for instance your views on Government do to me, and mine to you; but our dear Charles Stuart has entirely cured me of that and made me ashamed of it. While yet a boy I became acquainted with him, and from that time till now our intimacy has been almost that of an *indivisible existence;* and yet our creeds and speculative opinions, doctrinal views and philosophical belief are as wide asunder as the poles. We are always discussing when together and always disagreeing in opinion. . . .

WELD TO ANGELINA GRIMKÉ *

Feb. 8, 1838

. . .

I cannot close this letter without announcing to you a fact, the knowledge of which may *spare you much pain*. It is this. I have *no expectation* and almost no *hope* that my feelings are in *any degree* RECIPROCATED BY YOU. I have no doubt but you esteem me as a [C]hristian brother, respect me as a man of principle and feel as tho I had desired your welfare, and do heartily thank me for having faithfully pointed out your defects, however imperfect the mode of ministration; but that you have in the least degree any other feelings, I have no reason to believe, and as little assurance that the knowledge of my own feelings toward you may give birth to such feelings. If I were at all in a mood to philosophize on the subject, my inference would be that a disclosure so sudden and utterly unexpected on your part and withal so beset by seeming inconsistencies, would shock and repel you. But philosophy and policy and worldly wisdom and tact and dexterous maneuvering to carry a point have not been my counsellors. I eschew them all, and in conclusion I cannot refrain from saying that this whole matter has been infinitely far from *my own seeking*. When I found the strength of my affection for you, I strove against it till weary with conflict and convicted of sin. Whether the conviction was from above or from beneath, *another day will reveal*. It has often occurred to me that God might have ordered it in his providence as a crowning trial, to test my love to Him and see whether I would at His bidding cheerfully relinquish *all, but* Him and *for* Him. I need such a trial and if come it must, even so Father so it seemest good in thy sight. Tho' HE slay me yet will I trust in Him. If (and I have hardly a hope that it is otherwise) your heart, Angelina, does not reciprocate my love, I charge you before a risen Lord not to shrink for a moment thro fear of giving me pain from declaring to me the *whole truth*. If God call me to it I am *girded* for it and will, yea, I *can* and *will* come off conqueror. I can and will, yea, I trust I *have*, brought my insurrectionary

* In this letter Weld displays that uncertainty as to the proper course of action that plagued him as a reformer. His seeking of divine guidance and concern that he will not get it are evidenced often in his letters.

spirit into captivity unto the obedience of Christ. However I may be torn in the conflict, mine shall be the victory thro Him that loved me and gave himself for me. I can and will bear the burdens He layeth upon me; and however for a time they may bow me down, I shall rise again for the Lord upholdeth me. The cup that my Heavenly Father giveth me shall I not drink it? Yea verily I will *drain* it too, tho it be gall and wormwood. To God and the word of His grace I commit you and in submission to *His will* wait the issue.

THEODORE D. WELD

WELD TO LEWIS TAPPAN *

Dec. 14, 1841

As they are pressed with multiplied duties in the House on Committees, etc., etc., and have little leisure for gathering materials they request me to spend the winter there and aid them in the matter.

They have sent on money to bear my travelling expenses and will pay all my expenses while there, giving me access to the Congressional library, drawing for me whatever books and furnishing for me whatever facilities their *membership* puts within their reach. The letter is long and detailed; this is enough to show you its *scope*.

Now this request, coming in the shape and with the apparent earnestness that it does, oppresses me with the responsibility involved in the decision.

That those men are in a position to do for the A. S. cause by a single speech more than our best lecturers can do in a year, we all know. The fact that these speeches, prepared for the press by the speakers themselves after the delivery, will be published in the *National Intelligencer* or the *Globe* and thus scattered all over the south as well as the North settles that point. Further, not one of these men has been able fully to investigate the question of Slavery or any of the points upon which they propose to speak. The subjects are out of the range of ordinary congressional investigations and debates, the men

* Weld's difficulty in determining a proper course of action shows up in this letter, in which he rejects the third-party approach and instead turns to lobbying. Though he sounds confident this is the right course to follow, he soon changed his mind.

are all lawyers in large practice and have had no time for *thorough* looking at such matters; besides nothing that can help them on those points can be found in print, except in our Anti-slavery publications, and on *most* of those subjects we have either published nothing *at all* or nothing much to the point. On the whole the more I look at the subject the more I feel as though I *dare* not assume the responsibility of refusing to comply with such a request. Besides the immense good accruing from the speeches themselves, the fact that men NOT *sent* to Congress by the "*third* party" ("Liberty party") are ready to take *such ground*, will more than all things else open the eyes of abolitionists who far and wide are getting so intoxicated with third partyism and relaxing their grasp on the conscience of the South and the North.

WELD TO ANGELINA G. WELD AND SARAH GRIMKÉ *

Washington [D.C.] Jan. 9, 1842

MY DEAREST WIFE, AND DEAREST SISTER:

Your letter my dearest wife, mailed the morning of the 5th came to hand the evening of the 6th. The health, safety, peace and quiet of you all were a cordial to my heart and called forth thanksgiving to the merciful caretaker of us all. Oh how little do we take in of the length and breadth, the highth [*sic*] and depth of that love that passeth knowledge! My health is and has been ever since I came perfectly good. From nine in the morning till 3 in the afternoon I spend in the library of Congress *generally*, with the exception of about an hour from one to two o'clock when I run into the Senate or into the House of representatives for relaxation. Last Sabbath in the morning I went to the Capitol and heard one of the chaplains. Oh emptiness! Ephraim feedeth on the wind! Respecting the prophecies, beloved, and your fear that my mind is in an unteachable state respecting them: 1st. Blessings on you for your loving faithfulness in telling me of it and 2nd. that you have not suffered yourself to be swayed by my opinions, because they are *mine*. I know not what could sting me with

* Weld's admonition not to accept his views without the most careful prior consideration, and his warning not to expect some clear direction from God are further indications of the reformer's conviction that one must follow God's direction without any certainty as to where He will lead. This belief is evident in this and the letter that follows.

keener pain than the conviction that you and our precious Sarah were adopting *my* opinions on any subject without the most rigid examination, the fact of their being *my* opinions being *utterly without weight with you.* You are both well aware that I have often misgivings on this point, greatly fearing that your confidence in the general correctness of my opinions and in my habits of investigation might lead you to adopt my conclusions without that patient and thorough analysis, and without that independent investigation and scrutiny which is sacredly due to truth from all moral agents.

May God ever guard you here! As to the prophecies a single word. What is prophecy? It is the history of the future published before the occurrence of the events which it relates, or rather a statement of facts before their occurrence; and with refference [*sic*] to most of the prophecies yet to be fulfilled, I have little doubt that the only *clear* light in which they are to be read is that which will be reflected from the events themselves. Whether this is so or not, *this* at least is plain: Prophecy, whether it be the clear or the obscure foreshadowing of things to be, reveals no new attribute of God, no new element of man, duty or truth, or love, hope, trust, patience, peace or joy. Whatever combinations or affinities of *these* exist in prophecy, *there* is not the place to look for their *deepest* intensities. He that doeth my will shall *know* of the doctrine whether it be of God. When God leads the mind *to* the prophecies and *into* them, when God stimulates it to make them the subject of profound study, then duty is plain and *progress* will be as plain; but the history of the church shows that with few if any exceptions, great zeal for the study of the prophecies and little *practical spirituality* have gone together. The truth is, the study of prophecy has great witchery over minds of a certain cast. It powerfully stimulates curiosity, love of the marvellous, the element of superstition, the spirit of adventure, the desire for novelty, etc. All these powerful elements and tende[n]cies of human nature are set in a blaze when the study of prophecy is zealously taken hold of; and with how many does the mere constitutional zeal and sympathy excited by them pass for holy breathings! Satan's grand delusion I doubt not! Now my beloved I do not contend that prophecy is *never* to be studied, but that *God* is *first* to be studied, and so studied and communed with as to have the soul taken into captivity, moulded, filled with him; its principle, its tastes, its tendencies, its habits, its intensities so incorporated with the mind of

Christ, and *it* with them, as to secure that subjection and allegiance and vital union with him which ushers into the fullness of God. Then it will follow whithersoever God leads. It will never break a *path for itself,* but every step will be under God's pioneering. Dearest, Oh let us press on for this, press on to reach GOD. His light will lead us into all truth. Blessed be God for this promise "I will pour out my spirit upon you. I will MAKE KNOWN MY WORDS UNTO YOU." . . .

WELD TO SARAH GRIMKÉ

Jan. 15[?], 1842

My heart blesses you my precious sister and blesses God for your most tender self-denying and faithful labor of love in your letter which came to hand just after my last was mailed. Oh may it be an excellent oil which shall not break my head. Whether your opinion as to the *causes* be accurate or erroneous, this, at least, I know to be true. All the pride and impatience which you lay to my account, yea, *more far more,* IS MINE. The pride I have always been aware of; the impatience is a monstrous fungus growth of the last two years. Like a tropical plant in a hotbed, it has sprung up into a fearful strength, and oh how deep it has struck it[s] roots! *Mine* MINE is the guilt and the shame. Dear precious Sarah what shall I say to you! Oh pray that the fire that feeds on my spirit and burns to its deepest foundations may utterly burn up its baseness and purge it from earth. For more than two years I have ceased to know myself. Terrific visions have risen before me and haunted me everywhere and forever; but though the baptism has been with coals of fire, blessed be God, a sweet hope begins to dawn upon me, that it is to be a baptism unto life and not unto death. Pray Pray for me!

YOUR OWN THEODORE

Suggested Readings

Good surveys of organized pre-Civil War reform activity are Alice Felt Tyler's *Freedom's Ferment* (rev. ed.) (New York: Harper & Row, Publishers, 1942); and Merle Curti's *Growth of American Thought* (New York: Harper & Row, Publishers, 1951). Both authors view reform as an aspect of democratic liberalism. In more recent works a number of historians have related reform to religious interest. Especially good are John R. Bodo, *The Protestant Clergy and Public Issues, 1812-1848* (Princeton, N.J.: Princeton University Press, 1954); Whitney Cross, *The Burned-Over District* (Ithaca, N.Y.: Cornell University Press, 1957); Clifford Griffen, *Their Brother's Keepers* (New Brunswick, N.J.: Rutgers University Press, 1960); Timothy Smith, *Revivalism and Social Reform in Mid-Nineteenth-Century America* (Nashville, Tenn.: Abingdon Press, 1957); and Ray Billington, *The Protestant Crusade* (rev. ed.) (Chicago: Quadrangle Books, 1964). Among the articles dealing with the general reform impulse, David Davis's "Some Themes of Counter-Subversion," *Mississippi Valley Historical Review,* **47**, 2 (September, 1960), 205-24; and John Thomas's "Romantic Reform in America, 1815-1865," *American Quarterly* (Winter, 1965), 656-81, are especially challenging.

Historians have studied all major reform movements. Anti-slavery is best analyzed by Gilbert Barnes, *The Anti-Slavery Impulse* (rev. ed.) (New York: Harcourt, Brace & World, Inc., 1964); Russel Nye, *Fettered Freedom* (East Lansing, Mich.: Michigan State University Press, 1949); and Louis Filler, *The Crusade Against Slavery* (New York: Harper & Row, Publishers, 1960). David Donald's *Lincoln Reconsidered . . .* (New York: Random House, Inc., 1956) contains a chapter that interprets abolitionist motive. Donald's findings are challenged by Robert A. Skotheim in "A Note on Historical Method," *Journal of Southern History,* **25** (August, 1959), 356-65. Dwight L. Dumond's *Anti-slavery: The Struggle for Free-*

dom in America (Ann Arbor, Mich.: University of Michigan Press, 1961) is also valuable.

Temperance activity is best described and analyzed by John H. Krout, *The Origins of Prohibition* (New York: Alfred A. Knopf, Inc., 1925); and E. H. Cherington, *Evolution of Prohibition in the United States* (Westerville, O.: American Issues Publishing Co., 1920).

There are biographies of four of the five reformers considered in this volume. William Lloyd Garrison has been the subject of numerous studies: most useful are John Thomas, *The Liberator* (Boston: Little, Brown and Company, 1963); and Russel Nye, *William Lloyd Garrison and the Humanitarian Reformers* (Boston: Little, Brown and Company, 1955). The only biography of Theodore Weld is by Benjamin Thomas (New Brunswick, N.J.: Rutgers University Press, 1950), while Parker is the subject of a biography by Henry Steele Commager (rev. ed.) (Boston: Beacon Press, 1960). Constance Rourke's essay on Beecher in *Trumpets of Jubilee* (rev. ed.) (New York: Harcourt, Brace & World, Inc., 1963) is the best we have. Neil Dow's career has been traced by Frank L. Byrne in *Neil Dow, Prophet of Prohibition* (Madison, Wis.: University of Wisconsin Press, 1961). In all these biographies, Thomas, in his study of Garrison, shows the most concern to discover what motivated the reformer. The historians who have studied reform in general, rather than those who have dealt with specific movements, have done the best job of searching for motives.

The best way to understand what sort of people these reformers were is to study their own writings. Readily available are some Theodore Weld letters in Gilbert H. Barnes and Dwight L. Dumond, eds., *The Letters of Theodore Weld, Angelina Grimké Weld and Sarah Grimké*, 2 vols. (New York: American Historical Association, 1934); F. P. Garrison and W. P. Garrison, *William Lloyd Garrison, 1805-1879*, 4 vols. (Boston: Houghton Mifflin Company, 1894); Barbara M. Cross, ed., *The Autobiography of Lyman Beecher* (Cambridge, Mass.: Harvard University Press, 1961); and Neil Dow, *Reminiscences . . .* (Portland, Me.: Evening Express Publishing Co., 1898). Theodore Parker's sermons have been collected in a number of volumes.